Biochemistry Applied to the Brewing Processes – Malting

by

R. H. Hopkins

Copyright © 2011 Read Books Ltd.
This book is copyright and may not be
reproduced or copied in any way without
the express permission of the publisher in writing

British Library Cataloguing-in-Publication Data
A catalogue record for this book is available from
the British Library

Beer Brewing

Brewing is the production of beer through steeping a starch source (commonly cereal grains) in water and then fermenting with yeast. Brewing has taken place since around the sixth millennium BC, and archaeological evidence suggests that this technique was used in most emerging civilizations including ancient Egypt and Mesopotamia. Descriptions of various beer recipes can be found in cuneiform (the oldest known writing) from Mesopotamia, where the brewer's craft was the only profession which derived social sanction and divine protection from female deities, specifically: Ninkasi, who covered the production of beer, Siris, who was used in a metonymic way to refer to beer, and Siduri, who covered the enjoyment of beer.

The basic ingredients of beer are; water, a starch source, such as malted barley, which is able to be fermented (converted into alcohol), a brewer's yeast to induce fermentation and a flavouring, such as hops. Homebrewing, brewing on a domestic level has been done for thousands of years, but has been subject to regulation and prohibition during some time periods in certain places. One of the earliest, modern attempts to regulate private production was the Inland Revenue Act of 1880 in the UK which required a 5-shilling homebrewing license. Restrictions on homebrewing were lifted in the UK in 1963, Australia followed suit in 1972, and the USA in 1978, though individual states were allowed to pass their own laws limiting production. In some countries such as New Zealand, homebrewing beer or wine has always been legal.

There are several steps in the brewing process, which include malting, milling, mashing, lautering, boiling, fermenting, conditioning, filtering, and packaging. In general, brewing beer at home is very similar to brewing commercially. Homebrewers can select from ingredients identical to those used in commercial brewing, in addition to a wide range of post-market customization. But, in general, a hopped wort is produced and yeast pitched into the wort to stimulate fermentation. The complexity of the process is mostly determined by the approach used to manufacture the wort; by far the simplest and most commonly used method is 'kit brewing', obtainable from many high-street stores.

Whether the homebrewer chooses to mash his or her own grains or chooses to purchase malt extracts, the liquid will then need to be boiled, and the hops added. The length of time the wort boils with the hops varies, depending on the style of beer being brewed but overall boil times are usually an hour. Hops are added at different times during the boil, depending on the desired result. Hops added at the beginning of the boil contribute bitterness, hops added in the last thirty minutes contribute flavour. Hops added in the last few minutes or even after the end of the boil contribute both flavour and hop aroma. Finings such as Irish Moss, a form of seaweed, and others can be added in the final 15–30 minutes of the boil to help prevent haze in the resulting beer.

After primary fermentation, the beer may be moved to a secondary fermentation vessel to allow the beer more time to clarify and to reduce the possibility of off flavours due to dead yeast bodies and other sediment. Secondary fermentation is often when brewers choose to add flavouring agents like orange peel, oak chips or even more hops (so-called 'dry hopping'). Flavourings can include sugar, vegetables, herbs, spices, chocolate, coffee, or even a chicken!

People homebrew for a variety of reasons; it can be cheaper than buying commercially equivalent beverages, and allows people to adjust recipes according to their own tastes. Many enjoy entering homebrew competitions, sometimes referred to as 'craft brewing', and homebrewing has developed various clubs and competitions. In Britain, the 'National Association of Wine and Beer Makers' (amateur) and the 'National Guild of Wine and Beer' judge and sanction homebrewed beers, meads and ciders, offering categories for adjudicating. The national association have held an annual show every year since 1959. We hope that this book will inspire the reader to brew some beers of their own. Enjoy!

MALTING

The Chemical Composition of Barley

A typical two-rowed barley will have a composition approximating to that of the example shown below:

COMPOSITION OF TWO-ROWED BARLEY

	As stored, per cent	Dry matter, per cent
Water	12	—
Starch	56	63
Proteins	9	10
Comprising—		
Leucosin (albumin, water-soluble)	0·35	0·4
Edestin (globulin, salt-soluble)	2·8	3·1
Hordein (gliadin, alcohol-soluble)	3·25	3·6
Glutelin (insoluble)	2·6	2·9
Fats	2·5	2·8
Cellulose	4·3	4·8
Mineral substances	2·6	2·9
Comprising—		
Phosphoric acids	1·0	1·1
Silicic acid	0·75	0·85
Potash	0·6	0·65
Magnesia	0·25	0·3
Pentosans	8	9
Other nitrogen-free substances	5·6	6·2
Comprising—		
Mono- and disaccharides (1–2 per cent), lignin, tannins, pigments, bitter-resins, phytin		

The percentages of starch, protein, and pentosans may vary by 2–4 per cent from the above mean values, thus protein (on dry matter) may be as low as 7 per cent or as

Malting

high as 14 per cent. With higher total protein the *proportion* of hordein is higher, that of salt soluble less than indicated in the table.[43, 47]

It has been the aim of many scientists to find one or more measurable properties of the barley from which it might be possible to draw conclusions as to the properties of the resultant malt. No such analysis has yet been devised or is likely to be found, the qualities and properties of a malt sample depending upon the conditions during malting as well as upon the properties of the barley. When a standard malting method has been agreed upon it may perhaps be possible to draw conclusions from an examination of the barley as to the quality of the standard malt, but not of *any* malt made from the barley.

The starch is the most valuable constituent of the barley corn; the more starch, the more extract to be expected from the malt. However, there is no strict parallel between the two quantities, because proteins, pentosans, and other constituents of the barley enter into the malt extract. The microscopic appearance of barley starch is like those of rye and wheat starches and mixtures must be identified by means of impurities from the husk (hair, etc.). Liquefaction on heating with water takes place quite gradually, but the bursting of the granules occurs at about $65°–70°$.

The proteins are represented by the four typical groups of plant proteins. In the husk and aleurone cell layers the glutelin and the hordein predominate, whilst the water and salt-soluble proteins, leucosin and edestin, respectively, are found mainly in the so-called histological protein in the endosperm between the starch granules. The fat or ether soluble fraction which is liquid at room temperature consists of genuine glycerides of fatty acids together with about 25 per cent lecithin. Furthermore, a small quantity of sterols is contained in the fat, most of which is found in the aleurone cells and in the embryo.

The main part of the cellulose is contained in the husk

together with hemicelluloses (pentosans), but all the cell walls of the corn—including those of the endosperm—contain more or less cellulose.

The mineral substances are found partly—in small quantities—as constituents of amylopectin, phytin, and nucleic acids, and here phosphates predominate, and partly in the husks and other cell layers, where silicates predominate.

Mono- and disaccharides seem to be present mainly in the aleurone cells. Tannins and bitter resins, which tend to give rise to and may be detected by a disagreeable taste, are found especially in the husks.

If the starch granules in the endosperm are enclosed in proteins, hemicelluloses, or similar intercellular substances, the endosperm will look grey and "steely" if cut through, while the appearance will be white and "mealy" if the space between the granules is filled with air. The "steely" grains *of a given sample of barley* will therefore contain more nitrogen than the "mealy" grains,[1] but one sample of barley with many "steely" corns may very well contain less nitrogen than another sample of "mealy" barley.

In barley some vitamins of the B group and traces of vitamin A are found. Vitamin C is present only after germination has commenced.

General Conditions Necessary for Germination

Freshly harvested barley normally has a poor germinative power. The grain seems to contain certain substances which are slowly oxidised during the autumn, and only when this oxidation is complete is germination possible. If such grains are dried or steeped in dilute hydrogen peroxide,[2] or if the husk is removed so as to permit air (oxygen) to penetrate the grain the full germinative power is immediately developed —a fact which is sometimes utilised for the determination in advance of the true germinative power of a sample of barley.

Barley retains its germinative power almost unimpaired

Malting

for two or three years, provided the storage conditions are good. (These include low moisture content, avoidance of extremes of temperature, and absence of injurious substances or organisms.) After that time it decreases rapidly, and, after six or eight years, the germinative power will be only a fraction of the original.

In order to start germination suitable conditions respectively of *temperature, oxygen pressure,* and *moisture content* are required.

Barley can germinate at a temperature only a few (four or five) degrees above zero, but growth is extremely slow. With increasing temperature growth is accelerated and, on the whole, the optimal temperature is between 20° and 25°. The different processes, however, have not quite identical optimal temperatures, as will be seen later. According to Sachs, germination will not begin above 38°,[4] but if started at a lower temperature growth will continue even up to about 45°. If kept at this temperature with high water content, the plant will quickly die, but considerably higher temperatures can be survived if the main part of the water is first withdrawn.

Determinations of the air pressure necessary for commencement of germination of barley have shown that the limit is about 1/10 atmosphere.[3] For higher plants in general it is known that no growth is possible without any oxygen, and that oxygen pressures considerably below the normal generally inhibit both growth and germination. The special effect of low oxygen pressures upon respiration is dealt with in section 22.

Oxygen pressures above the normal seem to stimulate germination, but are harmful to the young plant in the long run. Pure oxygen has a more pronounced action than compressed air. Thus the influence of air at 5 atmospheres pressure on barley seedlings proved to be only slight and growth was not stopped until the pressures were higher than 10 atmospheres.[3]

Biochemistry Applied to Malting and Brewing

If temperature and oxygen pressure are at suitable values, barley will germinate when the water content is about 25 per cent or more.[4]

The essential feature of germination is the building process, but this building requires the presence of building materials and of available labour, i.e. chemical energy for the syntheses of new substances, and the production of these requisites is also a part of germination. Thus the whole of germination may be divided into four groups of processes, namely, (1) respiration, which furnishes the seedling with energy for the syntheses, (2) the *production* of enzymes, which catalyse the cleavage of reserve food substances and probably also the building of new cell materials, (3) the *functioning* of the enzymes, i.e. the *metabolic* changes brought about by their action, (4) the growth of root and acrospire. [Metabolism comprises all the chemical changes involved in physiological processes, and includes the breaking down processes (katabolism) as well as the synthetic processes (anabolism).]

Besides these, there is the very important process of absorption of water, the water content being the decisive factor in starting germination. Though the absorption of water is not a germinative process, the behaviour of barley towards water and the steeping process is naturally treated among the other germination processes, and most conveniently after respiration.

Respiration

(a) Normal Respiration, or Aerobic Katabolism

The growth of plants involves the building up of new cells and tissues, and of the materials from which these are made. Primarily the origin of all such materials is, in the case of chlorophyll-containing plants, carbon dioxide obtained from the air, water from the soil, and the necessary minerals from the latter. By the process of photosynthesis sugars are formed, the energy required for the synthesis being derived

Malting

from sunlight. In obscure ways fats and proteins as well as carbohydrates are formed and function as food reserves. When a cell requires to build a new cell or to enlarge itself, it synthesises the new material from simple compounds obtained from these food reserves or other nutrients. The latter are degraded by enzyme action into the simple compounds, which can diffuse easily from cell to cell. Resynthesis follows at the place where it is required, but energy is needed for this. Such energy is obtained by the breaking down of suitable compounds such as sugars in the processes of respiration. This term covers more than the mere taking in of oxygen and expiration of carbon dioxide, although the total effect, with its energy liberation expressed in calories, may be summed up by the equation given in section 23.

Respiration may be regarded as consisting of two kinds, aerobic and anaerobic, the latter being akin to fermentation. In aerobic respiration, atmospheric oxygen is essential and is the final acceptor of all the hydrogen present in the organic compounds which are broken down, whereas in anaerobic respiration and fermentation compounds such as aldehydes usually function as hydrogen acceptors, the corresponding alcohols being formed. The details of the mechanism of breakdown of the sugar are not known with any certainty, but are probably the same for both types of respiration as far as the stage at which acetaldehyde is formed (see section 50—Alcoholic Fermentation).

Hexose → hexose phosphate → triose phosphate → pyruvic acid → acetaldehyde + carbon dioxide.

While the carbon dioxide is simply excreted, the fate of the acetaldehyde is still obscure. It is not accumulated and must in some way be transformed to CO_2 and H_2O, perhaps by being successively dehydrogenated, firstly to acetic acid, then two molecules of this in turn to succinic acid; this

Biochemistry Applied to Malting and Brewing

again to fumaric acid and this by fumarase (section 17) hydrated to malic acid. Malic acid is easily dehydrogenated to oxalacetic acid, which, by the action of carboxylases, again produces carbon dioxide and one molecule of acetaldehyde.[5,6] Thus, of the original two molecules of acetaldehyde, one is "oxidised" and the one left may start again with a new molecule. This scheme is merely hypothetical and only based upon the existence of the different enzymes in the plant and animal tissues, but some facts dealt with in the next section support the hypothesis as to the existence of a number of different acids as intermediate products of the sugar breakdown.

In the dehydrogenation of normal respiration oxygen is—directly or indirectly—the acceptor of the hydrogen, water being formed; the carbon is transformed into carbon dioxide, and the freed energy appears as heat, just as if the carbohydrates had been burnt in a calorimeter.

Ungerminated barley respires only slightly, the amount being dependent mainly on the moisture content.[7]

Moisture, per cent	Mg. CO_2 expired in 24 hours per kg. dry weight at 20°
10–12	0·35
14–15	1·4
19–20	3·59
33 (germination setting in)	2,000

Temperature also has a great effect, the respiration with 10–12 per cent moisture at 50° yielding 15 mg. CO_2.

As germination proceeds the respiration increases vigorously,[8] water and carbon dioxide being produced in large quantities; the malt "sweats," and the accumulated carbon dioxide gradually inhibits the normal respiration. To remove the carbon dioxide and to cool the malt, it is turned (or in pneumatic maltings), the malt is artificially ventilated. The heat produced during the days of most intense respiration—the third or fourth day of growth—is

Malting

considerable, amounting to about 4,000 kg. calories per 100 kg. barley in twenty-four hours.

(b) *Abnormal Respiration, or Anaerobic Katabolism*

If a respiring plant or plant tissues are kept in a closed vessel, the concentration of the oxygen in the air is gradually lowered and that of carbon dioxide is increased. The case is often met with, and the change in conditions has a marked influence on the course of the respiration processes.

Even a slight increase of the carbon dioxide content of the air will reduce the expiration of this gas from germinating barley; evidently the action of the carboxylases of the seedlings is checked. But it is by no means stopped; carbon dioxide is expired steadily (but with decreasing velocity), even in high concentrations—20 per cent by volume and more—of carbon dioxide in the air. The absorption of oxygen, however, is not influenced by excess of carbon dioxide if only the oxygen pressure is approximately normal; this means that the dehydrogenation processes go on independently of the carbon dioxide in the air, and the various organic acids are steadily formed. As, however, the cleavage of the latter into carbon dioxide by the carboxylases proceeds more slowly than normally, an accumulation of acids in the cells must occur. This is actually the case, as is known from experience with the "CO_2 rest malting process" (Kohlensäurerast-malt) (see section 32). In this process the carbon dioxide is allowed to accumulate, thereby checking respiration and growth, but without hindering enzymic activity and modification. The acidity of the resultant green malt is found to be higher than that of normal green malt.

Normally, however, increase in carbon dioxide concentration of the air is accompanied by a decrease in oxygen concentration, whereby the conditions are further complicated. The influence is marked only at low oxygen pressures —below $\frac{1}{5}$ of the normal—the cells then lacking the natural acceptor for the hydrogen originating from the processes of dehydrogenation. The hydrogen therefore seeks other acceptors such as acetaldehyde:

$$2H + \underset{\text{Acetaldehyde}}{CH_3CHO} \rightarrow \underset{\text{Ethyl alcohol}}{CH_3CH_2OH}$$

with the result that alcohol is formed.[9] Possibly some of the many intermediate compounds formed are also acids reduced to the corresponding aldehydes, and these to alcohols. Certainly the seedlings accumulate all three groups of substances, and, furthermore, probably owing to the presence of esterases, esters are formed from alcohols and acids. These abnormal respiration products have, even in small concentrations, a pronouncedly toxic effect on the young plants. With very young seedlings this effect is quick and fatal, older plants may recover if oxygen is supplied afresh. Then alcohol, aldehydes, and acids are dehydrogenated with great energy, the esters are hydrolysed, and the cleavage products also dehydrogenated, the temperature is raised as a result of the strong "oxidation," the plant actually being febrile. If the plant is not supplied with oxygen it will, nevertheless, try to destroy the poisons with the only remedy at its disposal, viz. dehydrogenation. But without oxygen this will only make matters worse; dehydrogenating enzymes are produced in abundance and blindly attack various substances, the hydrogen reducing new compounds, and finally the plant dies in a chaos of uncontrolled enzyme processes.

The replacement of oxygen, as a hydrogen acceptor, by various aldehydes means *that respiration has been changed to fermentation*. As a matter of fact, seedlings or plant tissues cultivated in the partial absence of oxygen are able to produce alcohol and carbon dioxide in equimolecular proportions for some time,[9, 10] and it has even been possible to isolate active zymase preparations from such seedlings.

Malting

The Respiratory Coefficient

According to the equation,

$$C_6H_{12}O_6 + 6O_2 \rightarrow 6CO_2 + 6H_2O + 674 \text{ calories}$$

the volume of oxygen absorbed in the "oxidation" of sugar is equal to the volume of carbon dioxide expired. In the "oxidation" of fats, e.g. during the germination of seeds rich in oils, the low oxygen content of such substances as compared with sugars leads to a further consumption of oxygen, so that more oxygen is absorbed than carbon dioxide evolved. The ratio

$$\frac{\text{Volume carbon dioxide evolved}}{\text{Volume oxygen absorbed}}$$

is called the respiratory quotient and its value in the "oxidation" of carbohydrates equals 1, of fats approximately 0·7, and of proteins about 0·8. Some micro-organisms are able to live on oxalic acid or other oxidised acids, and in such cases the respiratory quotient is over 1·0.

Normally the respiratory quotient of germinating barley is very near 1·0, but if respiration changes from normal to abnormal, either through lack of oxygen or surplus of carbon dioxide, or both, the respiratory quotient increases. In a perfect (theoretical) fermentation the quotient would be infinite, but this value is, of course, never reached in practice. However, an analysis of the air surrounding the germinating barley will—especially in pneumatic maltings—frequently show that more carbon dioxide has been evolved than oxygen absorbed—indicating that abnormal respiration is going on. The determination is made simply by the methods of gas analysis, e.g. with an Orsats apparatus, but it must be remembered that, in the case of abnormal respiration, the sum of oxygen and carbon dioxide amounts to more than 21 per cent of the air (by volume) and the absorbed oxygen must, therefore, be calculated from the nitrogen percentage.

Biochemistry Applied to Malting and Brewing

Drying and Storage

Barleys, in countries with temperate climates, contain normally 16 per cent of water, in wet summers often more. If such barley is stored in bins, the heat developed by respiration raises the temperature in the centre of the bulk, from which heat cannot easily escape owing to bad conduction. Loss of vitality results. The water expired by the grains evaporates and is condensed in the outer, cooler layers. There it gives rise to excellent conditions for the growth of moulds and bacteria, and the parcel is soon spoiled. To avoid these difficulties, artificial drying on kilns or in drums at temperatures amounting to 52° is frequently resorted to. The water content is thereby reduced to 11 to 12 per cent, whereby respiration is reduced to a minimum, and the barley may safely be stored. An important incidental effect is that the germinative power is raised to a maximum at once. A further advantage is that if all barleys have approximately the same moisture content, when going into the steeping cisterns, this uniformity helps to simplify steeping procedure.

The temperature of the barley during drying should be regulated according to the moisture content. High temperatures cause damage to both vitality and enzymic activity the more easily the higher the percentage of moisture present. The results given opposite, due to Miller,[11] illustrate this, and also the improved keeping properties of dried barley.

Barley C had been previously dried *in vacuo* at ordinary temperatures to bring its moisture content down to 9·8 per cent. The results show that such barley withstood a temperature of 84° for twenty-two hours with only slight fall in percentage germination, whereas the barley containing 17·0 per cent moisture initially, showed a similar fall at 57° in four and a half hours, the fall in each case being calculated on the optimum percentage germination secured. However, a maltster would not risk heating his barleys to such high temperatures as would seem to be permissible for

Malting

two reasons: Firstly, an undiminished percentage germination is no sure indication that germinative activity and ease of modification have not been impaired; secondly, barleys may differ in their resistance to heat through causes independent of their moisture contents. Nevertheless, with barleys of low moisture content higher temperatures during

	Temperature, °C.	Final Moisture, per cent.	Time of Drying, Hours	GERMINATION AFTER STORAGE FOR	
				1 Month, per cent.	2 Months, per cent.
Barley A					
Raw barley ..	—	23·5	0	78	81
	46	8·4	17	99	98
	57	10·3	4·5	94	95
	66	10·9	2	94	90
	73	11·1	2	50	72
Barley B					
Raw barley ..	—	17·0	0	97	99
	46	7·9	17	100	100
	57	9·3	4·5	100	99
	66	9·5	2	97	97
	73	9·5	2	84	91
Barley C					
	—	9·8	0	92	97
	46	6·8	17	95	96
	66	5·7	22	100	99
	84	4·1	22	98	97

drying may be employed, and with progressive drying the temperature may be cautiously raised. Practical experience indicates that slow drying at gentle temperatures gives better results than hurried drying at higher temperatures. In all cases, storage after kiln or drum drying and before malting is an advantage. Great progress is being made and is to be expected by resort to vacuum drying of barley.[165]

Steeping

A water content of about 25 per cent is sufficient to start germination, but to secure normal growth without withering of the rootlets a much higher water content is necessary,

Biochemistry Applied to Malting and Brewing

and, therefore, barley is steeped until it *contains* 45 to 47 per cent water.

Air dry barley absorbs water with great energy, the vapour pressure of barley with 15 per cent water being about 5 mm. of mercury, which is the same as that of 50 per cent sulphuric acid. Under favourable conditions, such as in steeping, the absorption of water continues until the grains contain 47 to 49 per cent water. The velocity of absorption is highly dependent upon the temperature, as will be seen from the table below, taken from the results of A. J. Brown.[12]

TEMPERATURE, 34·6°		TEMPERATURE, 21·1°		TEMPERATURE, 3·8°	
Time, Hours	Water Absorbed, per cent.	Time, Hours	Water Absorbed, per cent.	Time, Hours	Water Absorbed, per cent.
5·00	16·80	5·25	9·32	5·58	4·42
24·00	35·64	24·33	24·80	24·75	11·82
48·25	43·44	48·50	35·98	48·83	18·52
71·50	45·36	72·00	43·42	72·25	23·42
96·00	45·74	96·25	46·90	96·50	27·42
				144·25	34·02

The absorption of water is accompanied by a considerable increase in volume due to the swelling of the substances which are hydrated. Neither this swelling, which proceeds with great force, nor the absorption itself (imbibition) are manifestations of life; dead grains will imbibe as well as living,[15] though perhaps not in just the same manner. The water diffuses into the undamaged corns through layers of living cells forming semi-permeable membranes, and normally no dissolved substances but only water is allowed to pass.[13, 14] From this point of view the composition of the steep water is almost without significance, though, of course, its biological purity must be beyond reproach. From the table it will be seen that the absorption of water proceeds quickly at the beginning, while the water is filling the capillaries of the outer layers of the grain and the space between the husk and the pericarp. If left in water too long the

Malting

barley slowly continues imbibition, but this last absorption is probably due to changes in the permeability of the membranes, for such oversteeped barley permits the passage of dissolved salts, acids, and bases into the endosperm and gives less uniform growth.

The velocity of the absorption of water varies considerably with the variety of the barley. Xerophil types grown in inland, dry areas swell and germinate more quickly than hydrophil types from maritime countries,[16] but still greater differences occur between the single grains. Uniform steeping throughout is obtained only with grains of uniform size.[16, 17] Since both under- and oversteeping have an unfortunate influence on the finished malt, the qualities of both malt and beer are to some extent dependent on the steeping process.

Understeeping is not really dangerous. The chief results are an abnormal growth of the rootlets, reduced respiration, and an incomplete breaking down of the proteins. The yield of malt is higher (less malting loss) than normal, but less extract is derived from it. Although the modification is not the best possible, the quality of the malt may be fairly good.

Oversteeping is much more dangerous. The danger arises not only from an excess of water, though this in itself has a bad influence. Barley can germinate and develop completely under water, if only the water is abundantly aerated, but in this case the development is quite abnormal, the acrospire growing with extreme speed and respiration being intense. However, in practice the most dangerous effect of oversteeping results from the lack of oxygen needed to keep pace with the exceedingly rapid respiration. With the imbibition of water respiration increases enormously. Thus 200 g. of Bavarian barley expired during steeping:[18]

From 0 to 7 hours ..	.. 38·4 mg. CO_2
From 24 to 31 hours ..	.. 84·9 mg. CO_2
From 48 to 54 hours ..	.. 183·0 mg. CO_2
From 72 to 78 hours ..	.. 248·0 mg. CO_2

Biochemistry Applied to Malting and Brewing

To secure normal respiration it will be understood that an abundant supply of oxygen must be available and abnormal respiration sets in if this condition is not fulfilled, poisonous by-products being produced in the corns. In the first stages of germination the seedling is very sensitive to these poisons and lack of oxygen at this period results in a high percentage of dead, ungerminated grains. Even if the seedlings survive, the febrile state afterwards disturbs the normal production and action of enzymes. Oversteeping manifests itself in the finished malt both by low extract content (due to the decreased action of the hydrolytic enzymes) and low yield (due to intense respiration). The malt is very heterogeneous, some grains being completely hard and unmodified, others with abnormally long acrospires. The wort is turbid because of the incomplete cleavage of the high molecular compounds, especially the proteins.

For the same reasons it is most important that air be admitted to the barley during steeping, the liquor being drained off at certain intervals or the water being aerated during steeping, whereby the barley is also washed and mixed.

As stated above, the composition of the steep water has no influence on the water absorption, but it may influence other processes such as the dissolving of certain substances present in the husk. The most important of these are tannin, bitter resin, and protein, all of which are deleterious to the quality of the beer; the first two by virtue of their disagreeable taste, the last because it is unstable in solution and gives rise to haze. All these groups, being of acid character, are dissolved the more easily the higher the pH of the steeping liquor. The most effective removal is obtained by steeping in lime water or other alkalies. The mixture of tannin, bitter resin, and protein has frequently been termed "testinic acid."

By such alkaline steeping more than 1 per cent of barley weight may be dissolved from barleys with coarse husk, of which 0·1 per cent may be recovered as "testinic acid,"

Malting

while fine husked barleys give considerably less.[19] Lüers has found that by alkaline steeping of coarse barleys a *definite improvement* in the quality of the beer resulted, but in the case of fine-skinned barleys either no influence or even an adverse effect.

The solubility in alkali of the husk constituents has been confirmed by Mündler, who observed an increased swelling of the corns, whereas steeping in acid solution gave less swelling and less extraction of "testinic acid."[20] Several experiments have been made by adding antiseptics to the steep water, such as bisulphite, hypochlorite, and even potassium permanganate.[20,21] The last two are supposed to stimulate germination because of their oxidising properties, but the main purpose is to kill all germs in the water and on the surface of the grains in order to reduce the growth of moulds on the floor.

The influence of variations of some conditions of steeping is summarised schematically below:

	Malt	*Beer*
Too much moisture (too long or too warm steeping)	Abnormal growth of acrospire, incomplete transformation of proteins, low extract	Tendency to haze
Too little moisture	High yield, transformation of proteins hardly complete, steely grains	Hardly any influence, perhaps a tendency to haze
Too little oxygen	Low yield, low extract, many ungerminated corns, incomplete protein breakdown	Tendency to haze
Alkaline steeping	Duller malt	Better flavour and taste, when not made from choicest barley

Biochemistry Applied to Malting and Brewing

	Malt	Beer
Steeping with antiseptics	Only of significance with long grown malt. Less mould on broken corns, therefore better flavour	Better flavour

The Formation of Enzymes

The various changes that take place during germination and which are comprised within the purely practical term "modification," include: (a) the morphological changes (growth of acrospire and rootlets); (b) histological changes (disappearance of the cell walls of the endosperm, and associated softening of the corn); (c) various metabolic changes, such as degradations of proteins, starch, etc., to simple diffusible substances; and (d) the formation and liberation of enzymes, to the activities of which all the other changes are due, either directly or indirectly. The formation of enzymes is therefore the first essential change within the corn which is about to germinate.

In the following survey of this enzyme formation the same consecutive order will be adhered to as has been and will be used later, viz. (1) carbohydrates or carbohydrases, (2) proteins or proteases, and (3) other substances such as mineral matter or the corresponding enzymes.

(1) Barley in the resting state contains small quantities of many enzymes. *Diastase*, however, is present in rather large quantity, though to some extent bound to proteins (hordein) in an inactive or insoluble form (zymogen). By digestion of ground barley with papain the extract obtained exhibits considerably greater diastatic activity than ordinary aqueous extract.[22] This is apparently due to the cleavage of the protein compounds. Barley diastase, both that which is soluble in water and that extracted with papain, is nearly pure β amylase (saccharogenamylase)[23] which transforms starch into β maltose (60 per cent), and a dextrin

Malting

(40 per cent), which gives a colour reaction with iodine. As regards the α amylase, sometimes a little but usually none is found in ungerminated barley, and barley diastase preparations possess correspondingly little power of liquefying starch paste.

It is by no means clear whether the liquefying power is to be identified with the α amylase. Evidently the latter, by breaking down starch into dextrins and maltose, will greatly decrease the viscosity of starch paste, and must be responsible for at least a part of the liquefaction. However, Waldschmidt-Leitz[25] has furnished evidence of the existence in malt of an amylophosphatase which is able to split inorganic phosphates from starch without saccharification, but accompanied by liquefaction.

During steeping and the very first stages of germination some of the β amylase activity seems to disappear, but after the third day of germination at ordinary temperatures more water soluble β amylase appears, apparently liberated by the action of the malt proteinase. The total amount, in general, is not increased more than 50 per cent during malting, but the proportion which is water soluble is more markedly increased. Rapid formation of active α amylase occurs during the third and fourth days of germination, concurrently with the increase in soluble and total β amylase.[24] The tables on p. 132 indicate the progressive appearances of these enzyme activities in the aqueous extracts. The rate of disappearance of the blue colour with iodine is taken to be a measure of the α amylase, as is also, with slight qualifications, the action on α amylodextrin (the residue unattacked by β amylase alone). The activity on starch measures the β amylase, although here again, with qualifications, since the α enzyme assists. Liquefying power was measured directly by Fletcher and Westwood[26] and by Lüers and Rümmler,[27] the results of the latter workers being illustrated by the graphs (Fig. 5), which represent (1) saccharifying power and (2) liquefying power. The dextrinising power, measured by a modification of the iodine reaction method, gave a curve almost identical with (2).

From Myrbäck:[24]

SAMPLE	Blue iodine reaction lost after		β AMYLASE Water soluble (Special units)	Total
Original barley	over	48 hrs.	15·9	18·9
Steeped barley	over	24 hrs.	13·6	20·9
Grown 2 days	about	20 hrs.	14·9	20·9
Grown 4 days	about	30 mins.	21·6	22·1
Grown 7 days	about	15 mins.	24·4	24·5

From Fletcher and Westwood:[26]

ACTION OF AQUEOUS EXTRACT OF 1 GRM. OF DRY GRAIN

SAMPLE	Grm. Maltose produced in 1 hour at 40° Starch	a amylodextrin	Liquefying power, grm. Starch liquefied in 1 hour at 21°
Original barley	—	0·4	4
At casting	—	—	1
1st day on floor	—	—	1
2nd day on floor	6·6	0·5	1
3rd day on floor	7·5	1·4	13
4th day on floor	12·1	2·5	42
5th day on floor	11·9	4·2	116
6th day on floor	16·1	4·9	140
7th day on floor	16·9	5·4	168
8th day on floor	14·8	6·6	174
9th day on floor	17·4	6·3	178
10th day on floor	17·5	6·8	160
Hand dried	10·3	5·1	168
12 hours after	9·1	4·8	198
24 hours after	6·4	3·6	214
36 hours after	7·2	3·2	208
48 hours after	5·3	2·6	214
At stripping	5·8	2·5	210

The diastase is produced only in the presence of oxygen[28] and mainly in the cells of scutellum, from which it diffuses into the starch containing cells of the endosperm.[29] The diffusion is made possible by the action of *hemicellulases* (cytase), which dissolve materials in the cell walls of the endosperm, leaving only a permeable skeleton. This process is the cause of the most evident feature of the modification of the malt, the softening of the grains. Lüers and Malsch[80]

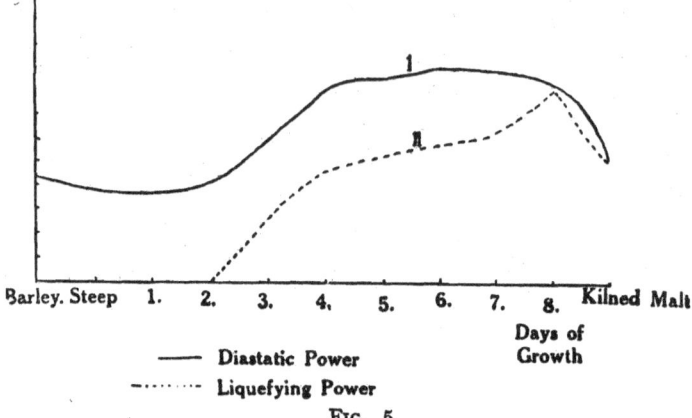

FIG. 5

CURVE I.—Development of diastatic power (β amylase) during malting.
CURVE II.—Development of liquefying power and of dextrinising power (α amylase) during malting.

have examined the production of hemicellulase by estimating the xylose formed by the action of an extract of the germinating barley on xylan (from elder pith):

	Mg. Xylose
Ungerminated barley	11·9
Steeped	7·9
2 days' growth	7·5
4 days' growth	18·7
6 days' growth	24·1
8 days' growth	28·0

The hemicellulase complex of germinating barley consists probably of a mixture of individual hemicellulases. Thus lichenase, which splits the hemicellulose lichenin into cellobiose, has been found in germinating barley by Karrer.

Of other carbohydrases the *maltase* must be mentioned. Evidence of its activity during germination is to be found in the observations of Brown and Morris,[29] and its presence has since been more clearly demonstrated.[31] It is so sensitive

Biochemistry Applied to Malting and Brewing

to reagents, alcohol, etc., that its actual isolation presents difficulties. It is apparently present to some extent in the ungerminated barley, and its activity is increased more than twofold during germination.[38]

(2) The *proteolytic enzymes* are rather difficult to estimate. Several investigators have found in germinating barley an enzyme of the *proteinase* type which acts on genuine proteins.[32, 33, 34] Its pH optimum seems to lie at about 4·3–4·6, and it must therefore be classified in the same group as papain. It is by the action of such that the β amylase is liberated during the first days of growth. Schjerning[35] has followed the transformation of the proteins by his special methods and from his analysis the following figures may be calculated.

	Grm. nitrogen dissolved during mashing, per 10,000 grains of Barley	Corresponding percentage of total Barley N.
Ungerminated barley	0·84	13·5
4 days' growth ..	1·88	30·0
7 days' growth ..	2·42	39·3
10 days' growth ..	2·48	39·8
12 days' growth ..	2·58	41·2

These figures, which refer to the combined action of the proteinase during germination and the mashing, may serve as an indication of the formation of the proteinase and as such they show that its production is already nearly complete by about the fourth day of growth.

The existence of at least two *dipeptidases*[32, 36, 37] in green malt has been proved, and possibly other peptidases exist. Their pH optima have been found to be as high as 7·9 and 8·5 respectively, but must depend to some extent on the substrate employed. They are also somewhat unstable to heat, etc. As the pH in growing barley and in the mash tun will never exceed 6·3, their action in the former will be limited and that in the latter, after the malt has been cured, will probably be nil.

(3) Of other enzymes only the *phytase* is of any practical

Malting

importance. It is present in barley to a very small extent, but is produced during the growth, the quantity in malt amounting to about ten times as much as in the barley. Green malt is a very popular raw material for the preparation of enzymes for scientific purposes, because almost all types are found and usually in relatively high "concentrations"; most of them, however, are only of theoretical interest. Most of the enzymes are formed during the first three or four days of growth, *and the formation is very sensitive to temperature, the optimum being probably about* 16° for the enzymes of practical importance.[35]

Metabolic Changes or Changes in Chemical Composition

The term "metabolic changes" is used here to signify *transformations in the materials present* (carbohydrates, proteins, etc.) by action of enzymes, that is, the work done by the latter as distinct from the formation of enzymes. Approximately 6·5 per cent of barley dry substance is soluble in cold water. This soluble matter is composed of substances of low molecular weight and these are used for the first building processes. In consequence they decrease in quantity during the first days of growth. When the enzymes are formed, new "low molecular" substances are produced by their action, and the content of water-soluble matter increases, as seen in the following table (from Lüers and Loibl):[38]

	Water Soluble Substances, per cent of Dry Matter
Barley	6·74
Steeped barley	6·48
1 day's growth	3·51
2 days' growth	5·07
3 days' growth	5·76
4 days' growth	9·88
5 days' growth	14·23
6 days' growth	14·26
7 days' growth	14·32

Biochemistry Applied to Malting and Brewing

The constancy of the values during the three last days indicates that the production of water soluble substances by the enzyme action and their consumption in the building of the seedling are proceeding at the same rates.

(1) The *carbohydrates* undergo changes that are small in quantity, though one of them is of great significance. The *starch* itself is attacked to a small degree by the diastase, its content falling by 4 or 5 per cent of dry matter during growth. The maltose thereby formed is immediately converted to glucose by the action of maltase. Glucose is partly used for respiration and partly transformed to fructose, and the two sugars condensed to sucrose, these three sugars forming the ready formed sugars of the malt. Lüers and Loibl[88] have studied the production during growth:

	PERCENTAGE OF DRY MATTER	
	Invert Sugar	*Sucrose*
Barley	0·380	1·86
Steeped barley	0·396	1·10
1 day's growth	0·244	1·56
2 days' growth	0·289	1·54
3 days' growth	0·727	1·98
4 days' growth	2·037	1·32
5 days' growth	3·114	3·70
6 days' growth	3·628	4·16
7 days' growth	3·344	4·95

It will be seen that the total quantity formed of these sugars is greater than the quantity of starch degraded. This is because some of them arise from the cleavage products of *hemicelluloses* from the cell walls of the endosperm by the action of the different hemicellulases (cytase). This process is very important and, next to the enzyme production, the main purpose of malting. The filtration of the wort in the mash tun requires a rather coarsely ground malt, and, if the cell walls of the endosperm have not been adequately attacked, the aqueous solution of the enzymes does not penetrate the particles; the starch is therefore incompletely converted and the extract yield is low. With fine grinding

Malting

this loss of extract does not arise, and therefore the difference between the extracts yielded by finely and coarsely ground malt will be an indication of the amount of cytase during malting. *Such figures constitute what is probably the best available measure of the degree of modification of malt.*

	DIFFERENCE, FINE–COARSE	
	per cent.	lb. per qr.
Malt, 2 days' growth	8·2	10·2
Malt, 4 days' growth	2·1	2·6
Malt, 6 days' growth	1·5	1·9
Malt, 8 days' growth	0·9	1·1
Malt, 10 days' growth	0·6	0·7

The soluble cleavage products of hemicelluloses, pectic substances, and other constituents of the cell walls of the endosperm form a part of the extract of the malt and consist mainly of hexopentosans. Loibl[38] and Fink[172] have found about 0·25 per cent of soluble pentosans in barley (dry substance) against about 1·2 per cent in malt. The cell walls of the endosperm are not completely dissolved, a fine skeleton, only visible in stained microscopical preparations, is left unattacked by the enzymes. Probably it consists of true cellulose.

(2) The *proteins* of the barley undergo considerable changes during germination. Firstly, by the action of the proteinase, which causes the first stages of degradation into soluble compounds, and then by that of peptidases, which catalyse the final cleavage to amino acids. The two processes have in the past been termed the *peptic* and the *tryptic* actions respectively, these terms being inappropriate, but, having a long tradition, are now and then still found in the literature. Of the total breakdown the most significant feature is that about half of the hordein is degraded into water soluble substances, some of which, later on, influence the physical properties of the beer and some serve as nutrients for the yeast. In addition, the total quantity of nitrogen is changed by the formation of the rootlets. In kilned malt without

Biochemistry Applied to Malting and Brewing

rootlets the nitrogen content of dry substance is usually 0·06–0·07 per cent lower than in the barley (say 1·43 per cent in the malt instead of 1·50 per cent in barley). Since malt dry substance is about 90 per cent of corresponding barley dry substance, this corresponds to a loss of 12–15 per cent of barley nitrogen, which corresponds quite well with a loss of 5 per cent rootlets containing 4·8 per cent N—thus no nitrogen is lost in other ways. Various investigators have examined by special methods the changes from day to day, but only the final results are of direct interest.

The following table gives typical compositions of the nitrogenous matter of barley and the corresponding malt. It should be remembered, however, that the percentage of total barley (and malt) nitrogen present as salt soluble and alcohol soluble will depend on the total barley nitrogen (see section 19). The proportion soluble on mashing the malt also depends on variety and on the original nitrogen content (see section 31).

BARLEY AND MALT NITROGEN PRESENT IN VARIOUS FRACTIONS, EXPRESSED AS PERCENTAGE OF TOTAL NITROGEN, TYPICAL TWO-ROWED BARLEY

	APPROXIMATE FIGURES		
	Barley	Malt (without rootlets)	
	Percentage of Barley N	Percentage of Malt N	Percentage of Barley N
Total N (= 1·6 per cent) ..	100	100	87–90
Soluble in cold water	17–25	25	22
Soluble on mashing (Congress)	—	50	45
Soluble on mashing and boiling (Congress)	—	43	38
Soluble on mashing (infusion 65°)	—	38	34
Soluble on mashing and boiling (infusion 65°)	—	35	31
Salt soluble (5 per cent K_2SO_4)	31	56	50
Alcohol soluble (70 per cent)..	34	17	15
Insoluble (glutelin N) ..	35	27	24
Formol N soluble in cold water	2	5	4·5
N assimilable by yeast ..	4	17	15

Malting

The transformation of the proteins seems to take place mainly during the third, fourth, and fifth day on the floor, that is just before the steep increase in diastatic power—indicating that diastase liberation is probably associated with this transformation. It will be remembered that the insoluble β amylase of the barley is associated with the hordein fraction, i.e. the fraction chiefly attacked.

The *fat content* falls during growth, the content in barley being about 3 per cent of the dry substance, whilst that of malt is only about 2·25 per cent, the decrease is probably due to respiration.

(3) Of the *mineral constituents* only the phosphates undergo changes of any importance. The phytin of the barley is split by phytase, yielding a mixture of primary and secondary phosphates with a pH value of approximately 6. The pH is not altered from barley to malt, whereas the buffer action, measured by titration with alkalies and phenolphthalein, or with acids and methyl orange, shows a considerable increase; thus Hopkins and Kelly,[39] using the electrometric titration, found the following values for germinating Norfolk barley, 1927:

BUFFER ACTION (C.C. N/10 ACID OR BASE PER 50 CORNS, NECESSARY TO CHANGE pH ONE UNIT)

	pH	Measured over range of pH		
		5·7–7·0	5·7–4·3	4·3–3·7
Barley	5·90	0·42	0·33	0·39
Steeped barley	5·20	0·23	0·22	0·26
3 days' growth	5·36	0·37	0·27	0·47
7 days' growth	5·98	0·55	0·28	0·49
9 days' growth	5·92	0·69	0·35	0·52
11 days' growth	5·87	0·69	0·35	0·52
45 hours on kiln	5·91	0·69	0·37	0·56
Finished malt	5·88	0·69	0·35	0·53

According to Prior and to Schjerning the soluble mineral matter is not altered, both in barley and malt 55–60 per cent of the ash is soluble.

Biochemistry Applied to Malting and Brewing

A review of the properties of growing barley is given below in two tables of analytical data from samples of malt taken at two-day intervals and dried as uniformly as possible on the kiln. Most of the figures result from an examination of the wort, and, in judging their values, due regard must be paid to the transformations during mashing. The worts were prepared by the Continental (Congress) method. The first table refers to a floor malting of pure cultivated (Danish) Binder barley of the 1925 crop, and the second to a pneumatic malting of pure (Danish) Kenia barley (1933).[168]

The extract increases during the first days as a result of more intense enzyme action, but later it falls because of the increasing respiration and the growth of acrospire and rootlets. The diastatic power also reaches its maximum in five to six days, but modification as measured by the difference, fine–coarse, is a much slower process. The appearance of the wort in the first sample of the last table is good probably because of the low content of "high-molecular nitrogen" (and the slow filtration). As the proteolysis proceeds the wort at first becomes more turbid owing to the high content of "high molecular nitrogen," but on continued hydrolysis the large molecules are broken down and the wort becomes clear. The surfaces tension varies correspondingly. At first it is rather high because of low content of surface active substances, then it falls to a minimum, then increases steadily because the cleavage products (small molecules) are less surface active than the "high molecular" proteins. The products of these changes give a better stability against haze formation but a poorer head retention capacity, as is well known from experience with over-modified malts. The decreasing viscosity adds to this effect. The colour of the wort progressively becomes darker as the malt is getting richer in the substances which produce and determine the colour, amino acids, and simple sugars.

Malting

(All results on Moisture Free Malt)

	FLOOR MALTING (BINDER)				PNEUMATIC MALTING (KENIA)				
Growth—Days	2	4	6	8	2	4	6	8	10
Extract, per cent	75·4	77·0	76·8	76·5	70·4	77·6	78·8	78·8	78·3
Equivalent to lb. per qr.	94·0	96·2	96·0	95·6	88·0	97·0	98·5	98·5	97·9
Difference fine—coarse extract, per cent	—	—	—	—	8·4	2·0	1·1	1·0	0·6
Equivalent to lb. per qr.	—	—	—	—	10·5	2·5	1·4	1·2	0·7
Diastatic Power (Windisch–Kolbach units)	61	120	126	127	99	148	168	175	175
Diastatic Power, degrees Lintner	22	39	41	41	33	47	53	55	55
Saccharification time, minutes	50	15	15	15	35	10	10	10	10
Colour of Congress wort c.c. N/10 iodine	0·26	0·38	0·40	0·43	0·18	0·21	0·24	0·25	0·30
Equivalent to degrees Lovibond on 10 per cent wort	3·0	4·4	4·6	5·0	2·1	2·4	2·8	2·9	3·5
Appearance of wort (turbidity in nephelometer)	Turbid	Slightly turbid		Clear	55	105	43	32	30
Filtration of wort	—	—	—	—	Very slow	Slow	Normal	Normal	Normal
Total nitrogen of Congress wort, N × 6·25 per cent	—	—	—	—	2·2	3·3	3·5	3·7	3·8
Permanently soluble nitrogen in wort, N × 6·25 per cent	2·8	3·1	3·5	3·7	1·9	2·8	3·1	3·3	3·3
Formol nitrogen in wort, N × 6·25 per cent	0·9	1·2	—	1·2	0·6	0·7	0·9	0·9	0·9
Surface tension of wort (water = 1)	0·58	0·56	0·57	0·62	—	—	—	—	—
Viscosity of wort (water = 1)	3·85	1·75	1·57	1·56	—	—	6·5	1	1
Steely corns in malt, per cent	—	—	—	—	100	14			

Biochemistry Applied to Malting and Brewing

The Building of New Tissues

Morphologically the most important process in germination is the formation of roots and acrospire, but from the point of view of the maltster these processes only cause a loss, because both are formed by synthesis of the valuable reserve substances. Under normal conditions the quantity of dry substance of the culms may be

	Percentage Barley Dry Substance
After 4 days' growth	1·32
After 7 days' growth	3·32
After 10 days' growth	5·64
After 12 days' growth	6·35

but these quantities may easily be reduced by various means, as will be shown later. The culms are utilised as fodder and their composition is, for instance,

	Per cent
Moisture	5·35
Protein	30·70
Fat	1·53
Mineral matter	6·23
Cellulose	7·08
N-free extract substance	49·11

Their nutritive value is considerable, corresponding to about 80 per cent of that of barley weight for weight.

The acrospires are left in the spent grains and are in themselves of no significance to the maltster and brewer. But the growth or length of the acrospire serves as an indicator of how germination is proceeding, and is, therefore, a valuable aid to the maltster in controlling the flooring. On the Continent the following lengths of acrospires are normal in the finished malts:

Fraction of Corn Length	Pilsener Malt Per cent	Munich Malt Per cent
Below ¼	2	2
½	23	8
¾	45	25
¾	29	56
1/1	1	9

Malting

A uniform development of the acrospire is evidence of a uniformity of germination processes, but it is not always possible to draw conclusions from the degree of development of the acrospire as to the development of enzymes and to their action in the cell walls of the endosperm. As already mentioned, excess of moisture will accelerate the growth of the acrospire without a corresponding acceleration of the other germination processes. Other conditions have a similar or opposite effect, so that on the whole *the length of the acrospire bears no certain relationship to the degree of modification of the malt.*

Influence of Variety and Quality of Barley on the Germination Processes and the Finished Malt

The different behaviours of various barleys during germination is, of course, always due to differences in chemical, physiological, and physical properties, but only in some few respects is the direct cause known. Considering firstly the germination processes we find the following.

The absorption of water is slower in the case of steely than of mealy or mellow barleys, thus Henlinger and Luff found for Bavarian barley:

Water percentage—	Steely Grains 11	Soft Grains 11	Steely Grains 17	Soft Grains 17
Before steeping	15·3	15·3	15·3	15·3
After 16½ hours	28·9	32·6	31·8	35·1
After 48 hours	37·6	40·3	41·0	43·0
After 72 hours	40·8	42·8	43·4	45·5

so that a longer steeping time is necessary for steely barleys. Otherwise the varieties seem to behave rather uniformly. Naked barley and winter barley absorb water at approximately the same velocity as ordinary barleys, provided the grains are otherwise alike and of the same size.

Respiration (and development of heat) is more marked with small-grained than with large-grained barley, simply

Biochemistry Applied to Malting and Brewing

because the former has the larger number of corns in a given quantity of barley. In addition, however, a high nitrogen content is usually accompanied by increased respiration, probably as a result of intense enzyme production.

The production of enzymes is dependent on both variety and growing conditions, but *on the whole* a high nitrogen content is usually accompanied by intense enzyme production, at least as far as diastase is concerned. The correlation often observed between the nitrogen content of barley and the diastatic power of malt is illustrated by the following table referring to pneumatic malt made from pure cultivated (Danish) Binder barley:[40]

Protein (percentage of Barley Dry Substance)	DIASTATIC POWER (Windisch-Kolbach units)	Lintner degrees, Approximate
9·8	169	53
10·0	184	57
10·3	187	58
11·0	200	62
11·9	207	64

and by the following results due to Bishop:[48]

Variety of Barley	TOTAL NITROGEN In Dry Barley, per cent	In Dry Malt, per cent	Diastatic Power, Lintner degrees	Colour, Lovibond degrees
Golden Archer ..	1·195	1·160	28	6·0
	1·363	1·340	33·5	4·0
	1·389	1·305	36	4·5
	1·389	1·336	32·5	6·5
	1·557	1·486	40	6·5
	1·580	1·360	37	6·0
Spratt Archer ..	1·213	1·136	28	6·0
	1·338	1·275	32	5·5
	1·358	1·297	30·5	4·5
	1·402	1·304	33	6·0
	1·599	1·526	42	6·0

Although the colours of the malts are not quite uniform, and a little allowance should be made (2–3° Lintner per

Malting

1° Lovibond) for this, the results are quite consistent with an increase in diastatic power accompanying increase in barley nitrogen.

Broadly speaking, the following connection between nitrogen content of barley and diastatic power of the *green* malt may be expected:

Nitrogen content, per cent	Protein content, per cent	DIASTATIC POWER	
		Windisch-Kolbach units, about	Lintner degrees, about
1·28	8	300	90
1·76	11	400	120
2·24	14	500	150
2·72	17	600	175

However, considerable deviations from these figures may be encountered, because the barley variety also has a pronounced influence on the production of diastase. Myrbäck[40] examined this question, using Swedish barleys grown under identical conditions, and containing similar quantities of nitrogen.

Barley	Protein	Diastatic power of Green Malt (special units)
Isaria	13·7	378
Binder	13·0	373
Kenia	12·9	265
Opal	12·9	222
Gold	13·0	191

The following figures from Thunaeus[41] refer to three barleys grown in the same place over a series of seasons.

DIASTATIC POWER

(*Windisch-Kolbach Units*)

Harvest	1929	1930	1931	1932
Binder	213	290	180	240
Opal	175	165	129	149
Gold	140	120	130	125

It is interesting to note that the above sequence of the

K

Biochemistry Applied to Malting and Brewing

five varieties coincides exactly with their value as malting barleys; Isaria is the best, Gold the poorest.

Of other enzymes only the catalase has been examined in malt of different barley varieties. Here Myrbäck finds *no* correlation between protein content and this enzyme, and *no* parallel between amylase and catalase contents.[165] Regarding this result it must be remembered that the two enzymes have very different functions in the growing seedlings, and therefore it is dangerous to draw the conclusion that there is no parallel whatever in the production of different enzymes. G. Krauss has found a certain parallel in the production of hydrolytic enzymes under varied malting conditions, and it seems reasonable to assume similar regularities with various barley types.

There seems to be little doubt that the *metabolic changes* (chemical transformations) during growth vary with the barley type, though the few quantitative examinations that have been made give but little information as to this point.

It is a well known fact that the modification of the malt depends to a high degree upon the variety. The number of steely corns in the malt may be used as a measure of modification, and the following table, from examinations of Swedish malting barleys by Thunaeus, shows the significance of variety.[44]

Barley variety	Protein in Dry Substance, per cent	Steely Corns in Malt, per cent
Isaria	13·7	3
Kenia	12·9	4
Binder	13·0	5
Opal	12·8	6
Gold	13·0	15

The changes in nitrogen fractions during malting are illustrated by the following table, taken from the results of Bishop.[42]

Malting

GRAMMES OF N PER 100 GRAMMES DRY MATTER

English (two-rowed), "Garton's Improved"

	SALT SOLUBLE				Alcohol soluble, Hordein	Insoluble, Glutelin
	Albumin	Globulin	Proteoses, etc.	Total		
Barley	0·186	0·159	0·223	0·568	0·631	0·509
Malt (no rootlets)..	0·184	—	—	0·935	0·269	0·393

Chilean (six-rowed)

Barley	0·215	0·165	0·220	0·600	0·568	0·580
Malt (and rootlets)..	0·145	0·275	0·435	0·855	0·425	0·550

A large increase in the salt soluble fraction, mainly due to increase in "globulin" and in proteoses and other degradation products, is approximately balanced by a substantial loss in the alcohol soluble (hordein) fraction, together with a minor loss in glutelin.

Hofman-Bang also has studied the changes in nitrogenous matter of different barleys and found as follows (unpublished results):[168]

	PERCENTAGE OF TOTAL N		
Barley variety	Salt Soluble N	Alcohol Soluble N	Decrease from Barley to Malt
Binder (a good malting barley)—			
Barley	36·7	36·7	15·4
Malt	50·2	21·3	—
Opal (medium)—			
Barley	35·4	35·2	12·5
Malt	51·3	22·7	—
Seger (poor for malting)—			
Barley	36·5	35·4	11·5
Malt	47·8	23·9	—

In both tables the quantities of alcohol-soluble protein transformed are greater in some varieties than in others of poorer malting quality.

As to the growth of *root and acrospires* also some variation will be found, as may be seen from Thunaeus's paper.[44]

Biochemistry Applied to Malting and Brewing

LENGTH OF ACROSPIRE

	0	<¼	¼	½	¾	⅞	>⅞
Isaria	0	4	7	38	50	1	0
Kenia	0	0	2	62	35	1	0
Binder.. ..	0	1	1	21	71	6	0
Opal	0	1	1	18	72	8	0
Gold	0	4	7	51	37	1	0

On the whole, however, the influences of the variety and composition on the different changes involved in germination are of less practical interest than the influences on the *quality of the finished malt*. This will be dealt with in sections 31 and 35.

29. Influence of Temperature on the Germination Processes and the Finished Malt

This question has been studied by Schjerning, who found the following *respiration losses* in ten days' growth:[57]

Floor Temperature	Percentage of Dry Substance
14	6·8
16	6·9
20	10·2
26	11·1

showing that respiration increases steadily with temperature, no optimal temperature being found within the range of temperatures employed. Data regarding *enzyme formation* are given in the table below, from G. Krauss:[58]

Floor Temperature	Diastase	Glycero-phosphatase	Nucleo-tidase	Autoproteolysis	Proteolysis by cleavage of Wittepeptone
14–15°	326	5·95	2·8	1·46	4·0
17–18°	315	4·65	2·3	1·46	—
24–29°	283	4·45	2·2	1·12	3·15

It will be seen that all enzymes are produced in smaller quantities as the temperature increases. The *metabolic or chemical changes* in the same three malts, as measured by

Malting

the difference between the cold water extract of the barley and malt, were:

Floor Temperature,	Extract	GRM. PER 100 GRM. BARLEY, DRY SUBSTANCE				
		Total	Nitrogen, Coagulable	Formol	P_2O_5 Inorganic	Organic
14–15°	9·4	0·31	0·05	0·13	0·102	0·097
17–18°	9·9	0·30	0·06	0·12	0·122	0·111
24–29°	9·4	0·23	0·05	0·08	0·111	0·094

It is most remarkable that the decrease in enzyme formation more than compensates for the increased action at the higher temperature. *A high flooring temperature gives the same metabolic or chemical changes (or less in the protein group) as a low temperature and a decidedly lower enzyme formation than the latter.*

It can be understood, therefore, that conversion during mashing is less complete in the case of warm grown than in the case of cold grown malts, as will be seen from a table on page 150. As to the *growth of rootlets and acrospire*, the following tables are illustrative:

FROM SCHJERNING'S LABORATORY[57] EXPERIMENTS
(10 DAYS' GROWTH)

Floor Temperature	Loss of Rootlets Percentage of Barley Dry Substance
14°	5·6
16°	6·1
20°	6·4
26°	5·1

FROM KRAUSS'S LARGE-SCALE EXPERIMENTS[58]
(7 DAYS' GROWTH ON FLOOR)

Floor Temperature	Average Length of Rootlets	Average Length of Acrospire
14–15	1·15	0·65
17–18	1·42	0·75
24–29	1·48	0·68

As regards Schjerning's figure for 26° it must be noted that the rootlets withered and stopped growth after the sixth day. The optimal temperature for the building processes seems to be about 25°.

The result of the influence of temperature of germination on the finished malt is seen from the following table of analytical data:

LABORATORY EXPERIMENTS (10 DAYS' GROWTH), SCHJERNING[57]

Temperature	Extract, per cent.	Acidity of 100 c.c. Wort, c.c. N/10 NaOH	CHANGE IN SOLUBLE Mineral Matter, per cent	CHANGE IN SOLUBLE Nitrogen (per cent of total)	Appearance of Wort	Overgrown (too long) Acrospires
14°	79·6	6·0	+2·0	+32·4	Extremely good	Some
16°	79·3	7·5	+5·5	+32·3	Extremely good	Some
20°	78·4	3·2	+2·1	+25·6	Very good	Many
26°	74·2	1·7	−1·0	+21·0	Good	Many

LARGE-SCALE MALTINGS AND BREWINGS, KRAUSS[58]

Temperature	Extract, per cent	Difference, Fine−coarse	YIELD IN MALTHOUSE, per cent	YIELD IN BREWHOUSE Percentage of Malt	YIELD IN BREWHOUSE Percentage of Barley	Saccarification Time, Minutes
14–15°	81·6	0·9	89·7	81·2	72·8	13·5
17–18°	80·0	0·6	87·8	78·8	69·2	15
24–29°	78·7	1·0	87·4	79·0	69·0	17

LARGE-SCALE PNEUMATIC MALTINGS, TUBORG[168]

Temperature	Extract, percentage Dry Substance	Difference, Fine−coarse	DIASTATIC POWER W.-K.	DIASTATIC POWER Lintner	Appearance of Wort
14–16°	80·7	1·5	87	30	Slightly turbid
18–20°	79·8	2·4	70	25	Turbid

Malting

Another example may be taken from Lüers[59] who made one malt ("cold") at a temperature varying from 13–15° throughout a malting period of ten days, and another ("warm") at temperatures starting at 14°, rising to about 24–25° in about seventy-two hours and kept there for the following six days. On examination of the malts he found:*

	EXTRACT (CONGRESS), PER CENT			Saccharifica- tion Time, Minutes	Diastatic Power, W.-K. units	Colour, c.c. N/10 Iodine
	Fine	Coarse	Difference			
Cold ..	81·4	80·4	1·0	12	416	0·22
Warm ..	80·3	79·2	1·1	10	376	0·20

	SOLUBLE Substance (grm. per 100 grm. dry matter)	N	Coagulable N (per 100 grm. dry substance)	Rootlet Loss, per cent	Respiration and Steeping Loss, per cent
Cold ..	6·374	0·527	0·131	4·32	5·4
Warm ..	5·953	0·483	0·145	4·03	9·3

In judging the beers made from such malts Lüers states that for Pilsener types the "cold" malts were decidedly the better, whilst for beers of Munich type the "warm" malts gave the better results, the beers in this case possessing fuller and more malty flavours than those made from "cold" malt.

Finally, an examination of the influence of "cold" and "warm" malting on the finished beer by A. Schmidt[60] may be cited:

	Attenuation, per cent	Total Protein in Beer, mg. per 100 c.c.	Formol "Protein" in Beer, mg. per 100 c.c.
Cold malting ..	62·5	443	23
Warm malting ..	62·2	392	19

	Flavour	Head Retention	Stability
Cold malting ..	Mild, palate-fulness best	7 (best)	24 days
Warm malting ..	—	45	16 days

Whilst agreeing that for the production of pale malt, germination at low temperature (14°–16°) is necessary or desirable, Krauss and Lüers find that the use of warm

Biochemistry Applied to Malting and Brewing

malting, i.e. germination at over 20°, whilst giving unsatisfactory results as regards the malt analysis, nevertheless when brewing Munich type of beer, gives satisfactory results so far as the beer is concerned. There is, however, no definite experimental evidence on the latter point, as beer properties, particularly flavour, are difficult to record numerically.

The general conclusion to be drawn from the experiments recorded above as well as from innumerable experiences in practice, is that vigorous enzyme formation and thorough modification are obtained only in cold malting, and that in general cold malting is the safest procedure to adopt.

The optimal temperature for a ten days' malting period, according to Schjerning, is a zone from 13° to 17°. Very fine barleys may also give satisfactory results in warm malting but always with greater loss. *In the case of barleys of poorer quality cold malting is imperative, and insufficient enzyme production and modification resulting from a short growing time cannot be made good by higher temperatures.*

Influence of Other Factors on the Germination Processes and the Finished Malt

Schjerning examined the influence of varied aeration, moisture, and light, with special regard to the protein cleavage, which he followed by his special and very laborious methods. As to the first factor (the principles of which have been treated in sections 21 and 22) Schjerning states that lack of oxygen causes a disturbance in the protein breakdown, with the result that the wort contains "albumin II." Further, he found the following figures on examining three malts grown under varied conditions of aeration.[57]

		PERCENTAGE OF DRY SUBSTANCE	
Malt grown 10 days with	Rootlets	Respiration Loss	Extract of Malt
Insufficient aeration ..	3·1	3·6	75·65
Normal aeration	4·1	5·9	77·79
Abundant aeration ..	5·6	6·9	79·61

Malting

Malt grown 10 days with	Malt Yield, percentage of Barley	Increase of Soluble N, percentage of total N	Appearance of Wort
Insufficient aeration	90·1	22·4	Poor
Normal aeration	86·8	26·7	Good
Abundant aeration	84·3	32·4	Very good

Whilst abundant aeration led to a malt yielding a high extract, the malting loss in this case more than compensated for this. It must be emphasised that such striking results are hardly obtainable in normal malting practice, where the aeration cannot be varied to such extremes as in Schjerning's experiments. The high yield due to the low losses in case of limited aeration has, however, led to the development of the "carbon dioxide rest" method of malting, which will be treated in section 32.

Variations neither in atmospheric humidity nor in light had any significant influence on growth except with regard to acrospire. In abundance of humidity or light the acrospire develops abnormally quickly, thereby, of course, influencing the yield. On the other hand, the losses by respiration and rootlets were slightly reduced if the air was either too dry or too moist. The enzymic processes, too, were somewhat retarded, but no directly abnormal result was recorded. Mention should be made of a special treatment of growing barley which has been tried lately. As already explained, variations in the composition of the steeping liquor will have no influence on the interior part of the grain, but, from the moment when the rootlets appear, their cells will be very sensitive to external influences such as high concentration of salts or abnormal pH in the film of water on the grain. Thus *sprinkling with acids*[61] should reduce the growth of the rootlets considerably and, at the same time, cause typical changes in the protein transformation. In this way a high yield is obtained and the malt is rich in soluble (and salt soluble) protein; furthermore, the content of formol

Biochemistry Applied to Malting and Brewing

nitrogen is increased, as a result of lower consumption in the building up of the rootlets.

Quite another treatment is used in the preparation of "enzymic malt," which is made by steeping the finished green malt in lactic acid. After drying, sufficient lactic acid is retained in the malt to cause a strongly acid taste and an almost complete destruction of all enzymes. On adding 3–5 per cent of this product to the grist in the brewhouse the pH of the mash will be lowered about $0 \cdot 2$, thereby favouring enzymic action during mashing, a method of practical value in countries where direct addition of lactic acid is prohibited.

The influence of the most important factors in practical malting or malt manufacture on the properties of the finished malt are summarised in the table, page 155, which is based mainly on the work of Schjerning, combined with practical experience.

Valuation of Barley

For the valuation of barley it is most important to know as far as possible the connection between the various properties of barley and the associated qualities of the malt and beer made from it. In both respects, but particularly as regards the latter point, very little is indeed known with certainty, mainly owing to the fact that the valuation of beer, which is, of course, the true criterion of both that of malt and that of barley, is hardly yet expressible in figures.

Below, however, an attempt is made to define a good malting barley and to state the optimal values of its properties as expressed by the results of a physical and chemical examination. As far as possible this attempt is based upon experimental evidence, and only where such is missing or has yielded contradictory results has regard been taken to general conclusions or practical experience. No attention has been paid to traditional assumptions

Malting

	Increasing Protein in Barley	Increasing Growing Time	Increasing Temperature	Increasing Aeration
Extract in malt	Falling	First increasing, then falling	Falling	Increasing
Extract yield, in terms of barley	Falling	First constant, then falling	Strongly decreasing	Decreasing
Diastatic power	Increasing	Increasing, then constant	Decreasing	Unaffected
Modification	More difficult	Increasing	Poorer	Better
Proteolytic activity	Increasing	Increasing	Slightly falling	Slightly increasing
Colour of wort	Increasing	Increasing	Unaffected	Slightly decreasing

Biochemistry Applied to Malting and Brewing

Apart from certain requirements, not concerned with physical and chemical characters, such as *a high germinative power, a good and sound smell, purity from weed seeds,* and *careful threshing,* which, of course, must be fulfilled to yield a high-class malt, a good malting barley must possess the following (biochemical) properties:

(a) *It must contain very little of the harsh and bitter tasting substances present in the husk.*
(b) *During germination it must produce ample hydrolytic enzymes, especially hemicellulases and proteases.*
(c) *It must yield a high percentage of its dry substance as "extract" after malting and mashing.*

As shown in a preceding section (28), the transformations during germination depend considerably in their quantitative manifestations on the *barley variety*. Actually the normal quality of certain varieties will generally satisfy the above conditions, thus being particularly suitable for malting, whilst other varieties will never, even in the finest condition, be able to give a high yield of good malt. The first postulate to be made is, therefore, that the barley belongs to a reputable malting variety and that it contains only this variety. Even a mixture of good malting varieties may give unsatisfactory results, because they may germinate at different rates. The fact that pure cultivated barley varieties (either pure race or selected hybrid) have been introduced in the malting trade in several countries is fully justified and a step towards safety for the maltster. In such countries a content of 5–8 per cent of another variety is usually not objected to, whilst higher percentages of impurities are not tolerated.

In case of a new variety with which practical experience is lacking it must be admitted that a physical and chemical examination gives only little information as to its value as a malting barley. With such a variety only an experimental malting[45] will give full information in this respect.

With a given variety of recognised malting qualities,

Malting

however, it is possible to judge samples of barleys grown in different places and under different conditions by an examination in the laboratory. As a guide for such examinations some correlations between barley properties and malt or beer qualities are given on the following pages.

(1) *The size of grain* plays an important part. The husk and surface layers of the grain are of no value to the brewer (apart from their action as filtering material), on the contrary, Lüers's examinations[19] of the husk constituents afford evidence that this part of the grain is rather of negative value to the brewer. The valuable matter lies in the inner part, and its relative quantity is mainly determined by the volume of the grain. The ratio surface : volume of a mass of particles increases with decreasing size of the particles. If any particles be broken into smaller ones, fresh surfaces are exposed without change in total volume. Surface is proportional to the square, volume to the cube of the diameter. Therefore, the smaller the barley corn the larger the ratio surface : volume or of deleterious or useless husk to extract yielding interior. Therefore, *large-grained barleys are of much greater value to the brewer than small-grained barleys—they give higher yield of extract and finer flavour.* The size of the corns is conveniently measured and their *uniformity* indicated by the Steinecker sieve, this dividing the sample into four fractions distinguished by the widths 2·8, 2·5, 2·2 mm. On the Continent barley parcels with more than about 10 per cent corns under 2·5 mm. are disliked, and in any case the small grains are removed in special screens before steeping. One thousand corn weight may also serve as an index of average grain size.

(2) *The nitrogen (protein) content* influences the yield of extract and the properties of malt, wort, and beer in several respects. It is a long-established experience that barleys with a high nitrogen content are difficult to grow on the floor, showing considerable germination without a corresponding modification. Bishop has shown that the malting

loss increases with increasing nitrogen content,[49] and, furthermore, he has proved that the extract content of the malt itself depends upon the nitrogen content and the thousand corn weight of the barley as expressed by the following formula:[50]

$$E = A - 10\cdot 5\,N + 0\cdot 20\,G$$

E being extract in brewers' pounds per quarter, A is the varietal constant (for English barleys about 107–110, for Californian 98–103), N the nitrogen percentage, and G the thousand corn weight in grammes, all quantities referring to dry substance. If the extract content is expressed as percentage determined by the Congress method, the constant and the factors must, of course, have other values. Bishop[51] has arrived at the following expression, based on a relatively small number of analyses and therefore provisional:

$$E = A - 0\cdot 85\,P + 0\cdot 15\,G$$

(where $P = N \times 6\cdot 25$)
and states a value for A of 83·0. Subsequent analyses of Bohemian barleys and malts by Novotny and Karabec[52] seem to indicate the value 83·6 as being more correct in the case of the type of barley in question.

Thus since the malting loss increases and the extract content in the malt itself decreases *with increasing protein in the barley, the total quantity of extract obtained from a given quantity of barley decreases markedly.*

As to diastatic power it must be remembered that a good variety of malting barley was characterised as being required to produce hydrolytic enzymes adequately at the same time as a high yield of extract, i.e. in spite of a low nitrogen content. However, the dominating influence on the diastatic power of the finished malt is the kiln drying, the importance of the nitrogen in this respect thus being relatively small.

For a given variety of barley the soluble nitrogen and the

Malting

formol nitrogen in the wort will increase with increasing barley nitrogen, being roughly proportional to the latter.[48, 53] But whilst good malting barleys will yield a high proportion, poor malting varieties will give a relatively low proportion of these two fractions. Thus from Thunaeus's and Schröderheim's[41] examinations of Swedish malting barleys it will be seen that the good malting variety, Binder, gives about 44 per cent soluble nitrogen in the wort, calculated on total malt nitrogen, whilst the poor variety, Gold, gives about 37 per cent. This means that wort from a Binder of 1·5 per cent nitrogen will contain about as much nitrogen as a wort from a Gold of 1·8 per cent, a fact that underlines the importance of the variety. In fact this percentage of the total malt nitrogen which is soluble in the Congress extraction has been proposed as an index of the modification of the malt, for instance by Schjerning, who considered 33 per cent soluble nitrogen in the wort calculated on malt nitrogen as minimum, indicating poor modification, whilst 50 per cent was considered the upper limit corresponding to rather over-modification. Kolbach[46] agrees in this, fixing the limits between 30 and 47 per cent. In worts prepared by the British (Institute of Brewing) standard method (10 per cent wort prepared at 65·5°) the corresponding figures are necessarily lower than those found in Congress worts, in the preparation of which special opportunity is given for proteolysis at 45°. For British barleys the *permanently soluble nitrogen* in the wort whilst varying is normally about 35 per cent of the total nitrogen of the barley and only slightly higher in terms of malt nitrogen, whilst with six-rowed Californian barleys the percentage is about 29.[47] All in all it will be seen that the quantity of nitrogenous matter in the wort depends as much on the variety as on the total nitrogen of the barley. Of course the method of malting also is liable to be of great influence, as may be illustrated by some figures selected from an examination of German barleys and the malts, worts, and beers made from them:[53]

Biochemistry Applied to Malting and Brewing

Total N in Barley (the Barley being Malted in different Maltings)	FORMAL N. MG. PER 100 C.C. WORT	
	Malt from one Malting	Malt from another
1·66	29·8	26·0
1·75	33·6	20·2
1·81	36·6	47·4

The functions and importance of the nitrogenous matter in the wort are treated in section 47, and it is evident from the foregoing discussion that these functions may very well be obtained with a low nitrogenous barley, when it belongs to a fine malting variety and is treated carefully during malting.

Only few observations have been made on the influence of barley nitrogen on the flavour and palatefulness of the beer, and, in fact, the evidence available (often merely opinions) is more or less contradictory, so that no definite statement is possible. Still less can be said as to the connection between barley nitrogen and the head retention and formation of haze in the beer on chilling, pasteurisation, or transportation—practical experience seems to indicate that all these properties of the beer are more dependent on the variety and the malting methods than on the total nitrogen in the barley.

Summarising, it must be admitted that very little clear evidence is available as to the influence of nitrogen content of the barley, but what little is known in connection with practical experience leads at the present time to the statement that *for pure or all-malt beers, whatever the type and whatever the gravity, barleys, supposed to be of a good malting variety, with low and lowest nitrogen should be preferred*, though, of course, this preference should not find its expression in unreasonably high prices. It must also be remembered that the wort obtained when using a barley of high nitrogen content need not itself be high in nitrogen since it may be diluted by the addition of maize, rice, or sugar to the grist. Actually the barley should not contain too little nitrogen if low gravity beers are brewed with a high percentage of raw grains or other malt adjuncts, for in this case, at least with

Malting

beers brewed on the British system, there may be shortage of assimilable nitrogen in the wort and difficulties may arise with the fermentation and yeast crop.

It is important, however, to be clear as to where the boundary line is to be drawn between what are considered high and low nitrogen respectively. The most commonly accepted figure on the Continent would be 1·68 per cent (or 10·5 per cent protein) on dry barley. In Great Britain, however, 1·5 per cent nitrogen would be regarded by most brewers as the border line.

(3) *The husks.*—Without doubt a quantitative determination of the percentage of husk would be of great value in the judgment of a sample of barley. A too high proportion of the bitter resins and tannins present in the husks is deleterious to the flavour of the beer, but, on the other hand, it has been found that beers brewed from naked barley or from malt flour were actually lacking in one element of the total flavour. A small content of these substances seems to give the very "keynote" of the beer flavour. The composition of the husks may, for instance, be[66]

	Per cent
Water	7·4
Protein	7·1
Pentosans	20·0
Fibre	22·6
Fat	2·1
Ash	10·0
Starch	8·2
Other N-free matter	22·6

the last-named group comprising also the tannin. Lüers isolated 0·2 per cent pure tannin, and the real percentage is undoubtedly considerably higher. The husks are present in the barley to an extent of 7–13 per cent, so that the tannin calculated on barley is at least 0·02 per cent; from a paper by Hartong[67] the content is calculated to about 1 per cent, a point to be remembered later in the discussion on precipitation of protein during wort boiling. There exists no convenient method for the determination of the quantity of husks in a barley; the only known way, separation by hand and weighing, is too elaborate for routine control. A rough estimation is made by simple observation, and the barley with the finest husk should, of course, be chosen.

It is worth noting that the husks contain less protein per cent than the whole corn, but no correlation can be made between the percentage of husk and of total protein. This is illustrated in the following table.

PERCENTAGE OF DRY BARLEY

BINDER BARLEY OF GRAINS[168] BETWEEN 2·5 AND 2·8 MM.		PLUMAGE-ARCHER (CANADIAN)[71]	
Protein	*Husk*	*Protein*	*Husk*
9·2	9·2	8·54	11·3
9·4	9·1	9·30	11·9
11·7	7·8	9·48	10·2
12·3	8·8	10·20	10·15
12·6	8·4	10·78	10·2

(4) *The moisture content.*—The value of a barley is proportional to its content of dry substance, and proposals to regulate the price accordingly have been set forth. However, any such simple correction for moisture would not be equivalent to the decrease in value, since the moisture content influences the properties of barley in several ways. Apart from the one mentioned, the size of the corns is increased with increasing moisture, thus giving the impression of quality better than the actual. As shown by Berglund[55] this effect may be of practical importance when barley is purchased with a guaranteed grain size. The smell may be influenced in a most disagreeable way by growth of moulds if the moisture exceeds 17–18 per cent; in this case the germinative power will also be impaired. In fact a parcel may be valueless for malting purposes because of too high a water content, while the correction in the price based on proportionality with dry substance would only give a reduction of some few per cent. Therefore, on purchasing barley

Malting

due attention should be paid to this factor. In practice, however, the difficulty is met with that the samples taken from the bulk are sent to the buyers often in paper envelopes or small bags, thus allowing artificial drying, and preventing effective control. As long as maltsters and brewers do not object to this type of sample the possibility remains open that an almost valueless lot of barley may be purchased, and at a high price. Further, damp barley *must* be kiln dried.

(5) *The colour.*—It is generally assumed that a light yellow colour of the barley is caused by good growing and ripening conditions, thus indicating good malting qualities, and this view is supported by the following examples[168] of the connection between colour of barley and analytical data of malt. Two lots of Binder barley grown on one farm on the same kind of soil in the dry summer of 1934 were purchased for malting in spite of rather poor quality, only because the one lot had happened to get some showers of rain while the other had not. The former was straw yellow, the latter yellow-white. After malting in exactly the same way the malts were examined with the following results:

	Malt from Yellow Binder Barley ($N = 1.92$ per cent dry)	Malt from White Binder Barley ($N = 2.03$ per cent dry)
Moisture	2·40	2·67
Extract (on dry substance), per cent	76·9	76·6
(equivalent to) brewers' lb./qr...	96·0	95·6
Difference fine/coarse, per cent	1·1	1·5
(equivalent to) brewers' lb./qr...	1·4	1·9
Diastatic power, W.-K. units	155	155
Diastatic power, Lintner	52	52
Saccharification time, minutes	10	10
Appearance of Congress wort	Turbid	Clear
Turbidity, nephelometer units	189	40
Colour of 10 per cent wort, Lovibond	8·8	6·1
Total N in wort, percentage of extract	0·70	0·72
Perm. Sol. N as percentage of extract	0·61	0·65
Formol N as percentage of extract	0·19	0·18

Thus there seems to exist in this case a correlation between barley colour and wort colour and turbidity, the latter point indicating a more thorough cleavage of high molecular substances during mashing of the malt from the white barley—otherwise there was no difference.

(6) *Steely corns* in a barley will generally, but not always, have a higher nitrogen content than mealy ones, although in any one case of two different barley samples the more steely may very well contain less nitrogen than the less steely. However, steely barleys usually require longer time for growth and, according to investigations of Ehrich,[56] give a higher malting loss than mealy barleys, but the finished malts are generally of equal quality if the protein contents of the barley have been equal.

(7) *The thousand corn weight*, as will be seen from Bishop's formula for predicting extract, has some influence on the extract yield of malt. Otherwise it does not aid essentially in valuing the barley.

As an illustration of the practical application of the principles of barley valuation discussed above, the valuation scheme used in the Tuborg laboratory is outlined on p. 165, together with two analyses of Danish barley.

Such properties as water content or germinative power, which have not necessarily the same values in a sample sent in paper or fabric as in the lot, are determined only in the latter. It will be noted that the above scheme may be completely filled in within one hour. The moisture content may be measured (electrically) in a few seconds. Thus a parcel need not be received before the valuation is finished. Usually parcels with less than twenty-five marks are not taken into consideration.

The Various Systems of Malting

The fact that systems of malting other than the "classical" floor malting have developed is not the outcome of indications of malt of better quality, but is entirely due to the

Malting

	Valuation in Marks	Abed Binder Marks 14		Abed Maja Marks 7	
		Per cent	Marks	Per cent	Marks
Subjective Examinations					
General impression (including variety)	Fine malting barleys as Archer, Binder, Isaria, etc., are given up to 15 marks, less fine (as six-rowed) up to 10				
Fineness of husk	Is marked from -5 to $+5$		1		2
Smell	Is marked from -5 to 0 (normal sound smell)		0		0
Colour	Is marked from 0 to 5		3		2
Objective Examinations—					
Size of grains—					
2·2 mm.	The percentage is multiplied by -0.3	(1·0)	-0.3	(1·0)	-0.3
2·2–2·5 mm.	The percentage is multiplied by -0.1	(5·4)	-0.5	(4·2)	-0.4
2·5–2·8 mm.	The percentage is multiplied by $+0.1$	(40·2)	4	(39·8)	4·0
2·8 mm.	The percentage is multiplied by $+0.3$	(53·7)	16	(55·0)	16·5
Protein (N × 6·25) in dry substance	11 per cent is regarded as normal (in Denmark) and marked 0. Every 0·1 per cent more counts -1 mark, every 0·1 less, 1 mark. With the less fine varieties this applies only down to 10 per cent, lower contents being all marked 10	(11·1)	-1	(9·7)	10
Steely grains	The percentage (by number) is multiplied by -0.05	(92)	-4.6	(98)	-4.9
Other grains than barley	The percentage by weight counts negatively	(0)	0	(0)	0
Damaged grains	Likewise	(2·2)	-2.2	(1·6)	-1.6
Germinated grains	Likewise	(0)	0	(0)	0
Sum of marks			29·4		34·3

better economy and greater efficiency of the mechanical methods. This does not mean that the quality of pneumatic malt is necessarily inferior to that of floor malt, but it is very difficult under otherwise equal conditions to get it better. In the preceding sections it has been shown that too much or too little of the various factors that influence the quality of malt results usually in one or more of the germination changes becoming abnormal and poorer malt results. It is easy to understand, therefore, that extreme conditions, even if they affect only a fraction of the grains, will lead to heterogeneous, low quality malt. This is liable to happen in some pneumatic maltings and is a fact which explains fully the predominance of floor malting. The uniform treatment of all corns secures a uniformity of modification in all its aspects which is so much appreciated in the brewery because it facilitates brewhouse technique and gives rise to no difficulties.

If in a pneumatic malting (e.g. drum, Saladin or Kropf) the grains are treated as individually and uniformly as in a well-conducted floor malting, the quality of the malt will be just as good, and in chemical physiological respects only few special considerations can be applied to any of the normal malting methods. The velocity of the germination processes is usually somewhat retarded in pneumatic malting, probably because of inhibited respiration, which again is caused by imperfect aeration in the deep layers of barley. The air usually follows channels along which evaporation is intense, while in the bulk of grains only a very slow replacement of the air takes place. This difficulty, perhaps combined with the high mechanical pressure in the lower layers of barley, causes a very slow growth of rootlets which, on the other hand, reduces malting loss. In Tuborg's pneumatic malting (Saladin boxes) a yield of 82 kg. malt dry substance on 100 kg. barley dry substance is very common with ten days' growth, while the figure from the floor malting is usually about 81 per cent, in spite of there being only six to seven days' growth.

Malting

In the Kropf malting system reduced aeration is utilised to the limit and the influence on the composition of the finished malt is very marked. The barley is steeped and grown normally for three or four days in the boxes, then aeration is reduced and the growing barley "rests" in an atmosphere of increasing carbon dioxide content. The reduced respiration and growth cause a high yield, but are followed by secondary consequences. Enzyme formation proceeds quite normally and is nearly finished before the *carbon dioxide rest*; during this process (in the last three days) the hydrolytic enzymes cause an almost normal breakdown of the reserve substances; but, as only very little substance is consumed for respiration, and as the growth of root and acrospire is almost stopped, a relatively large quantity of low-molecular compounds is *accumulated* in the grains, they are not *produced* in larger quantities than normally, but they are not used up for resynthesis. The substances in question are monosaccharides, amino acids, polypeptides, and inorganic phosphates. In practical malting the accumulation of these compounds increases the formation of colouring matter on kilning, because the latter is actually formed from simple sugars and amino acids on heating. Kropf malt is thus especially suitable for the brewing of dark beers, and, owing to its higher content of buffering substances such as phosphates and amino acids, for hard brewing liquor. Kropf himself, however, claims that typical Pilsener malt may also be made by his method. Some analytical results from a comparative examination of floor, drum, and Kropf malts by Lüers[62] are collected in the following table, to which are added some average figures for a typical English floor malting (from Ling).[63]

	TOTAL LOSS	RESPIRATION LOSS	LOSS AS ROOTLETS
	Percentage of Dry Barley		
Floor malt	11·31	5·35	4·46
Drum malt ..	10·25	4·93	3·82
Kropf malt ..	7·18	3·05	2·36
English floor malt..	8·3–10·0	3·5–4·5	3·0–3·5

Biochemistry Applied to Malting and Brewing

	Acrospires from ¾–1 per cent	Formol N in Green Malt (Millival in 40 grm. Dry Matter)	Total Acidity of Green Malt	Invert Sugar, per cent
Floor malt ..	78	5·57	3·39	1·90
Drum malt	74	5·00	2·43	—
Kropf malt	48	8·96	5·97	3·00
English floor malt..	88	—	—	—

Physiological and Chemical Processes during Kilning

The drying of the green malt on the kiln finally stops germination and the malt can now be stored. Furthermore, the character of the beer is determined both directly and indirectly. Colour and flavour depend directly on the kilning process, and the composition of the beer is determined by the action of the enzymes during mashing, which, again, depends on the kilning.

Both the chemical transformations of the green malt constituents and the survival of the enzymes are influenced strongly by the action of *heat* and *in the presence of moisture*.

The formation of enzymes is finished by the time that properly withered malt is brought on to the kiln and will in no circumstances start again. But the functionings of the enzymes continue and may do so with considerable effect, in spite of the fact that the enzymes themselves are seriously damaged by the higher temperatures. These two processes are especially favoured if the malt is kilned as for amber or dark malts, or for Munich malt, that is to say, only a slight draught being maintained during the lowest and the medium temperatures and the final temperature being rather high, e.g. above 100°. In such cases, therefore, the moisture content of the malt is kept high in the first hours, and the conditions are excellent for hydrolytic processes. The important hydrolyses of proteins and of starch proceed especially at the medium temperatures from 50° to 70°, thus giving rise

Malting

to an abundant formation of amino acids and simple sugars which form the raw materials for the production of colouring and flavouring matter. These enzyme activities in the presence of moisture are illustrated by the following table from Kolbach and Schild.[4]

	Water in Malt, per cent	INCREASE PER 100 GRM. MALT DRY MATTER IN 8 HOURS' DRYING				
		At 30°	40°	50°	60°	70°
Extract, grm. ..	23·2	—	—	0·4	2·3	3·4
	33·5	0·6	2·9	5·3	8·0	—
	41·9	2·0	4·2	9·7	—	—
Fermentable ex-	23·2	—	—	0·3	1·3	2·4
tract, grm.	33·5	0·7	2·1	3·1	5·8	—
	41·9	1·2	2·3	5·6	—	—
Permanently	23·2	—	6	56	138	124
soluble N, mg.	33·5	25	86	188	222	—
	41·9	41	100	244	—	—
Formol N, mg. ..	23·2	—	5	32	55	45
	33·5	15	46	93	93	—
	41·9	28	56	113	—	—

The high final temperature also is, of course, detrimental to the enzymes, and this all the more as the water content is still relatively high at 70°–80°. It will be remembered that enzyme preparations are the more resistant to heat the drier the preparation containing them. In these dark malts there remains only a small enzymic activity, represented by the most thermostable enzymes, viz. the amylase and the proteinase, while cytase, phytase, and peptidases are totally destroyed. Quite another system is followed in the kilning of ordinary (pale) malts. Here the main part of the water is removed by an intense draught at the lower temperatures, thereby inhibiting the hydrolytic processes and reducing the destruction of the enzymes. The final temperatures also are lower than for dark and coloured malts, viz. 89°–96°, normally, and for Pilsener malt 80°–85°, and these temperatures are easily resisted by most enzymes in the dry condition. As a matter of fact, if they are again soaked with water, a few corns may resume germination after a typical Pilsener kilning.

It will be seen that by suitable control on the kiln the enzyme content of the malt may be varied between all and nothing, but it is also possible to destroy such enzymes as are sensitive to heat without destroying others; thus the kilning may be controlled in such a way that the greater part of the β amylase is destroyed while the α amylase is left almost intact. As will be seen later, the ratio of these two enzymes has a pronounced influence on the course of the mashing processes and the composition of the wort and the beer.

The colouring and flavouring substances formed at the highest temperatures during kilning include compounds of unknown composition which are formed from monosaccharides and amino acids. The process is probably a condensation, but carbon dioxide is also produced in considerable quantities; the formation is very slow at temperatures below 100°—only at this and higher temperatures does the process proceed more quickly. Dry mixtures of amino acids and monosaccharides do not react, they must be both present in aqueous solution. In experiments with pure substances[64] it has been found that glucose, fructose, galactose, and especially arabinose react easily, forming, with glycine, strongly coloured products with a flavour like breadcrust, with alanine, similar products, with valine, less colour but a fine malt flavour; leucine gives a substance with intense bready flavour. The resulting substances have an acid (or perhaps amphoteric) character, they disperse colloidally in water, the particles possessing normally a negative charge, whilst those of normal beer colour are positively charged at the pH of beer (4–4·5). The coloured substances formed on the kiln from amino acids and monosaccharides are not the same as those of caramel, which is formed by heating sugars to 200° or more. They have quite a different flavour and are the principal colouring con-

Malting

stituents of coloured malts. The so-called caramel malt is produced by keeping green malt at a temperature of about 70° for some hours; a very thorough transformation of starch and proteins is thereby obtained, and sugars and amino acids are formed in large quantities. On heating to 110° or so an intense formation of typical malt flavour and colour takes place. It may be remarked here that a premature rise in temperature while grains still contain much water may give rise to the formation of vitreous corns through liquefaction of the starch. This type of vitreous corn is not of disadvantage as is undermodified malt. Indeed crystal and amber malts for brown ale brewing are purposely made in such a way.

On the kiln the malt may be treated in special ways. Thus, it may be sulphured by burning sulphur beneath the floor, whereby the sulphur dioxide disinfects and bleaches the malt. In some places the combustion products from wood are allowed to pass through the malt, which will thereby absorb a small quantity of phenols; the beer from such malt has a characteristic smoked flavour and is very stable against bacterial infection.

Some data illustrating the transformations on the kiln are given in the table on p. 172, representing results of analyses of malt samples taken from one piece at different temperatures during kilning, and mashed by the Congress method. The transformations during mashing are therefore involved in some of the figures.[168]

It will be seen that the extract content falls with increasing temperature, partly because some of the proteins are coagulated, but mainly because the β amylase is destroyed; this causes a low value of the ratio sugar: dextrin in the wort, which slightly reduces yield of dry extract. The partly coagulated proteins and incompletely degraded carbohydrates cause turbidity in the wort from the samples taken at the highest temperatures; these worts, of course, also have the darker colour, but it is interesting to note the

	At Dropping from Upper to Lower Floor 6·93	70° 4·77	80° 3·79	90° 2·57	100° 2·01	110° 1·36
Water, per cent						
Extract, percentage of dry malt	80·7	80·8	80·8	80·4	79·7	78·4
Equivalent to lb. per qr.	100·7	100·8	100·8	100·3	99·4	98·0
Appearance of wort	Clear	Clear	Clear	Slightly turbid	Slightly turbid	Turbid
Colour of wort (cc. N/10 iodine)	0·21	0·21	0·22	0·26	0·32	0·80
Equivalent to degrees Lovibond (10 per cent wort)	2·4	2·4	2·5	3·0	3·7	9·3
Total N in wort, as percentage of extract	0·76	0·77	0·80	0·79	0·75	0·72
Permanently soluble N in wort, as percentage of extract	0·68	0·68	0·70	0·70	0·68	0·60
Diastatic power (W.-K. units)	248	215	169	111	75	34
Equivalent to degrees Lintner	75	66	53	36	26	14

Malting

sudden increase in colour in the sample heated to 110°. The nitrogen content of the wort increases at first as a result of continued action of the proteinase on the kiln, but falls in the later samples because of protein coagulation, and reduced proteolytic activity during mashing. The quantity of permanently soluble nitrogen in the wort varies in parallel with the total. Finally, the diastase undergoes violent destruction at the highest temperatures.

These changes have a marked influence on the procedure of the subsequent brewing processes, the filtration time, the clarification of the wort and the attenuation, and, of course, the colour of the wort. These processes are dealt with in detail later, but a preliminary impression may be gained from the following table,[168] showing some properties of three uniformly made malts, cured at different temperatures.

Final Curing Temperature	Filtration Time	Appearance of Wort
80°	½ hour	Clear
100°	1 hour	Slightly turbid
115°	2 hours	Turbid

Colour of Wort, c.c. N/10 Iodine	Colour of 10 per cent Wort, Degrees Lovibond	Attenuation (apparent) per cent
0·20–0·22	2·4	82
0·60–0·70	7·5	77
1·30–1·40	15	73

The Finished Malt. Its Composition and Analysis

A proximate analysis of malt yielding percentages of starch, insoluble carbohydrates and fibrous matter, sugars, nitrogen, fats, mineral matters, etc., would be of very little use to a brewer. His main concern is the quantity and quality of the extract to be derived from the malt under the conditions of mashing employed by him. The quantity of extract is determined by an empirical process, either that agreed upon by the Salzburg Convention ("Congress"

Biochemistry Applied to Malting and Brewing

method) for decoction brewers or the method of the Institute of Brewing. The former and the methods of analysis generally employed on the Continent are described in certain textbooks,[166] and the latter and the usual British processes in the Journal of the Institute of Brewing.[167] The quality of extract is indicated by such determinations as nitrogen fractions, colour, etc., which are of some use in judging the value of the malt and can be very useful to the brewer.

The figures below may serve as examples of typical English malts:

	Pale Ale Malt	Mild Ale Malt
Moisture, per cent	2	2
Extract, lbs. per qr.	99	97
Cold water extract, per cent	18	19
Diastatic activity, degrees Lintner	35	28
Colour of 10 per cent wort, degrees Lovibond	4	8
Permanently soluble N, per cent	0·5–0·6	0·6
As percentage of total barley or malt N	33–40	33–40

Continental malts are analysed in a somewhat different manner, the so-called Congress method being employed. The two principal malt types are the Pilsener and the Munich type, of which typical analyses are given on p. 175.

According to recent investigations by Hopkins, Hind, and Day,[65] the following calculations for converting the results of British (Institute of Brewing) Standard Analysis to results which would have been obtained by the Congress method are appropriate.

Moisture	Add 0·23 per cent
Extract	Multiply by 0·802
Colour	Multiply by 0·086
Diastatic capacity	Multiply by 3·50, then subtract 16

(The last converts degrees Lintner into Windisch-Kolbach units.) In contrast to these technical analyses, a scientific

Malting

	Pilsener Malt	Munich Malt
Moisture, per cent	3.5	2.3
Extract, fine grind, per cent Plato	77.2	77.7
Extract, coarse grind, per cent Plato	75.95	77.1
Extract in dry substance, fine grind, per cent	80.0	79.5
Extract in dry substance, coarse grind, per cent	78.7	78.9
Difference fine-coarse, per cent	1.3	0.6
Odour on mashing	Fresh, green malt	Full, aromatic
Appearance of wort	Bright	Clear
Turbidity (nephelometer index)	20	40
Colour of wort, c.c. N/10 iodine	0·16–0·18	0·60–0·70
Saccharification time, minutes	Less than 10	10–15
Total protein in malt, per cent	9.9	9.8
Non-coagulable protein in malt, per cent	2.95	3.8
Diastatic capacity (W.-K. units)	330	100
Steely grains, per cent	1–2	0–1
Caramelised grains, per cent	0	2
Acrospires less than ½ length, per cent	2	1
Acrospires ½ length, per cent	25	5
Acrospires ¾ length, per cent	42	25
Acrospires ¾ length, per cent	27	58
Acrospires 1 length, per cent	4	11
Acrospires more than full length, per cent	0	0

analysis of a normal malt would give, for instance, the following results:

	Approximate percentage of Dry Substance
Starch	58
Reducing sugars	4
Sucrose	5
Soluble Pentosans	1
Insoluble pento- and hexosans	9
True cellulose	6
Proteins (N × 6·25)	10
Composed of insoluble	3
Salt soluble	5
Alcohol soluble	2
Non-coagulable	2·5
Formol (also N × 6·25)	0·7–1·0
Fats	–2·5
Mineral matters	2·5

In addition malt contains small quantities of colouring matter, inositol, bitter resin, tannin, etc.

The malt starch has almost the same appearance as barley starch, but may be identified by the granules being slightly corroded, due to an attack by diastase during germination. The temperature of gelatinisation is the same as for barley starch (62°–70°), though a true formation of malt starch paste is not normally seen because of the presence of the liquefying enzyme. The reducing sugars are mainly glucose and fructose, maltose being present only in very small quantities, probably because the malt contains the enzyme maltase which causes cleavage of the maltose to glucose. The reason for the presence of sucrose is rather difficult to understand, as is the process of its formation; as shown by Brown and Morris and other investigators, it is formed from maltose or glucose by enzymes in the embryo. The insoluble pentosans, cellulose and glutelin, form the dry substance of the spent grains which also contain the fat. It may be here pointed out that it is not very logical to insist that rice or maize for brewing purposes must not

Malting

contain more than 1 per cent fat (because of its detrimental influence upon head retention) since malt itself contains about three times as much. Of the different groups of nitrogen compounds the salt soluble fraction of the malt apparently contains all the nitrogen of importance to the brewing processes, and this group should be as high a fraction of the total nitrogen as possible. The mineral substances of malt are the same as in barley—except that a higher fraction of the phosphorus is present as inorganic phosphates.

The malt enzymes of practical importance are listed below in tabular form:

Enzyme	pH Optimum	Temperature Optimum
Amylophosphatase (individual existence doubtful)	about 4·7	65–70°
α or Dextrinogen amylase	5·7	65°
β or Saccharogen amylase	4·7	55°
Proteinase	4·3	50°
Peptidase I	7·8	40–45°
Peptidase II	8·6	40–45°
"Cytase" (several individual enzymes)	5·0	35–45°
Phytase	5·2	60°

These optima refer to laboratory experiments with aqueous extracts. Under mashing conditions the temperature optima are about 5°–10° higher, and the pH optima of starch and protein fission more alkaline, as will be shown later.

The last four enzymes are so sensitive to heat that they are only present in small quantities in low-kilned malt, and have not been detected at all in high-kilned types like Munich malt. Besides the enzymes in the above table, several other enzymes of mainly theoretical interest are present in low-kilned malt.

The vitamin content of kilned malt is much the same as that of barley, any vitamin C which was formed during germination having been destroyed during kilning.

Biochemistry Applied to Malting and Brewing

Valuation of Malt (see also tables, pp. 174, 175)

An examination of malt gives two views: one retrospective, i.e. backward through the malting processes to the barley variety and quality, the other forward through the brewing processes to the worts and in some degree to the finished beer.

(1) *The moisture content* will depend on the kilning and storage. In fresh malt conclusions may be drawn as to the maximum temperature of curing. During storage, without precautions, malt can absorb water up to (at least) about 12 per cent, when it will be in equilibrium with air of normal humidity. In the brewhouse the moisture content is of importance in two respects: firstly, the yield will be proportional to the content of dry substance; secondly, a rational grinding requires a suitable and low water content. In countries where duty is paid on the malt, the former point will, of course, dominate, whilst elsewhere the latter will determine the moisture. A very dry malt will be ground to flour, thus complicating the filtration (especially mash *tun* filtration). The best moisture content for normal grinding lies at 3·5 to 4 per cent water.

Brewers employing the infusion system of mashing as in Great Britain, will not use slack malt, i.e. malt containing over 4 per cent of water, although such malt, redried, is usually acceptable. In this method of mashing, the temperature attained within the first minute or two of the grist and liquor coming together is all important, as this infusion system involves virtually only one temperature for the whole mashing operation. The composition of the wort, particularly as regards nitrogen compounds, will be largely influenced by this temperature. But the latter is a function not only of the temperature of the grist and that of the liquor ("striking heat") and the proportions of these, but also of the heat evolved when dry malt is mixed with water. Such heat diminishes with increasing moisture content in the malt, so that a slack malt, mashed according to a routine

Malting

procedure, will yield a lower temperature at mixing than a normal malt. How far the disastrous results experienced when slack malt has been used are due to this cause and how far to other unexplained causes is unknown. It must be remembered that the ordinary redrying (torrification) process may be adequate for malt which is slack only in the husk and outer layers of the corns (malt which has only recently become slack), whereas malt which is slack right through the corns (a slackness acquired further back or through imperfect curing) may not be, adequately redried.

(2) *The extract* needs no further explanation; it should, of course, be as high as possible, though with due regard to the other properties. However, it is worth mentioning that the extract as given by the Congress or the British standard method is in no way the maximal extract obtainable from this malt. Partly because the grains from a laboratory mashing contain substances which may be dissolved on more thorough treatment (boiling, addition of diastase) and partly because the ratio maltose : dextrin in the wort influences the yield (specific gravity), it is quite possible to obtain a higher yield in a brewhouse working with intense methods (three mash method, Schmitz's method) or at lower saccharification temperatures than is found with a laboratory method.

(3) *The difference in extract, fine–coarse grinding*, is undoubtedly the best objective determination of the degree of modification, indicating as it does the permeability of the endosperm. However, it suffers from a considerable analytical error—the whole error of each determination being comparable with the difference between fine and coarse grinding. To obtain a reliable result it is necessary to make two fine and two coarse grindings. A high difference is associated with a poor yield of extract, and in extreme cases, slow filtration and turbid wort. The figures quoted in section 34 are the values aimed at in several Continental breweries; for infusion mashing it would probably be advisable to

demand lower differences, thus a difference about 0·3 per cent is frequently found in English malts.

(4) *Cold water extract or ready-formed soluble sugars.*—The latter quantity is usually arrived at by deducting four from the percentage of solids soluble in water at 21°. One or both of these determinations also give information as to the modification of the malt: the higher the figures, the more enzyme action on the floor. However, the values are mainly determined by the diastase, thus affording little information as to the more important enzymes in this respect, viz. the cytase and the proteases. For infusion mashing the ready-formed soluble sugars should be about 13–15 per cent of the malt, for decoction mashing 10 per cent will be normal. A higher figure indicates over-modification and is often accompanied by a corresponding excess of protein fission products, and is therefore an indication of much amino nitrogen in the malt. However, direct determination of the latter, viz. the percentage of the total malt nitrogen, which is (1) permanently soluble, (2) "formol" is more to the point. Altogether, the cold water extract determination, mainly used in Great Britain, is nowadays giving place to these latter determinations.

(5) *Appearance of the wort.*—The turbidity (when measured in a nephelometer) is an index, expressed in one figure, of the relative size and number of colloidal particles in the laboratory wort. On the whole, it is an indicator of the actions of all dissolving enzymes in the malt, such as diastase, hemicellulases, and proteinases. Therefore the kilning temperature is of great influence on the figure, the wort being more turbid, the higher the temperature, owing mainly to destruction of enzymes, but also to some coagulation of proteins. With a good quality of malt the following figures will be easily obtained (Congress wort):

Maximal kilning temperature	80°	85°	90°	95°	100°	105°	110°
Turbidity in Zeiss's Stuphophotometer	10	15	20	40	80	150	220

Malting

The barley variety is of great importance, poor malting varieties always giving much higher figures than fine malting barleys.

(6) *The colour of the wort* gives no information as to the *quality* of the malt, but is merely, taken in conjunction with the Lintner value, an indication of type, e.g. pale or dark. Increasing tint may be caused by far-driven modification, carbon-dioxide rest, much moisture on the kiln, high kilning and curing temperatures; and all these influences may be balanced by suitable variations of the others. The colour of the beer is just as much dependent on methods of mashing, wort boiling, cooling, and filtration as on the colour of the malt.

(7) *Saccharification time*, measured by the disappearance in the mash of blue colour with iodine, is actually no measure of saccharification but of disappearance of starch and formation of achroodextrins. A short saccharification time indicates a high activity of α amylase, which breaks the starch down to much dextrin and some α maltose, while the main part of the maltose (β maltose) is formed by the β amylase, which, however, does not cause disappearance of the iodine colour. Therefore a short saccharification time does not tell much of saccharification, particularly because β amylase may have been greatly restricted, whilst the α amylase is still active owing to its high thermostability. It is worth noting that a short saccharification time bears no relation to the final attenuation of the wort. In any case the saccharification time should not exceed twenty-five minutes for a Munich and fifteen minutes for a Pilsener malt.

(8) *Diastatic power.*—This determination is of great importance to the brewer who employs infusion mashing without rakes; in this case an adequate diastatic power (and a thorough modification) is very important. In decoction mashing or when the mash is otherwise stirred it is only necessary to have a high diastatic power when a low final attenuation is the objective—for this determination gives

information as to the sugar-forming capacity of the malt (as against the saccharification time) and bears a direct relation to the degree of attenuation. For the British infusion system about 24–40 degrees Lintner are desirable, whilst for the brewing of Pilsener lager beer the aim should be to secure at least 250 W.-K. units, and for Munich types about 100 W.-K. units. When grain adjuncts are employed, such as maize or rice, the diastatic power must be high enough to secure conversion of the adjuncts as well as that of the malt itself.

www.ingramcontent.com/pod-product-compliance
Lightning Source LLC
LaVergne TN
LVHW040743250326
834688LV00031B/423